The Way of Serenity

Finding Peace and Happiness in the Serenity Prayer

FATHER JONATHAN MORRIS

HarperOne
An Imprint of HarperCollins*Publishers*

HarperOne

THE WAY OF SERENITY: *Finding Peace and Happiness in the Serenity Prayer.*
Copyright © 2014 by Father Jonathan Morris. All rights reserved. Printed in the
United States of America. No part of this book may be used or reproduced in
any manner whatsoever without written permission except in the case of brief
quotations embodied in critical articles and reviews. For information address
HarperCollins Publishers, 195 Broadway, New York, NY 10007.

HarperCollins books may be purchased for educational,
business, or sales promotional use. For information please e-mail the
Special Markets Department at SPsales@harpercollins.com.

HarperCollins website: http://www.harpercollins.com

HarperCollins®, 📖®, and HarperOne™ are trademarks of HarperCollins Publishers.

FIRST EDITION

Designed by Terry McGrath

Library of Congress Cataloging-in-Publication Data is available upon request.

ISBN 978-0-06-211913-1

14 15 16 17 18   RRD (H)   10 9 8 7 6 5 4 3 2

Thank you, Francis, for teaching me
again that Jesus's way is simple: mercy,
humility, truth, and service

CONTENTS

INTRODUCTION

❧

I T WAS A frigid day in January. I thought my overcoat was buttoned all the way to the top, but a part of my clerical collar must have been showing. A man in his late twenties approached me on a short side street in Lower Manhattan, not far from Wall Street. He was anxious to let me know that he didn't believe in God. Jim was as kind and sincere as could be. He felt compelled to talk to me about his disbelief, not that I might convince him otherwise, but rather to let me know that he was working hard to be a good person even though he did not have faith in my God.

I was impressed by Jim's candidness and by his passion for communicating the truth that many nonbelievers are very, very good and moral people. I thanked Jim for feeling comfortable enough to approach me. I thanked him too for trying to live a virtuous life, and I told him he had inspired me to double-down on the same goal. Finally, I told him that, if he wouldn't mind, I would pray for him, and somewhat routinely and naively, I asked him to pray for me as well. Jim shook my hand, smiled kindly, and began to walk away—only to stop after several paces, turn around, and tell me something I would never forget.

1

"I don't really believe in prayer, because I don't know if anyone is listening, but I do really like that 'Serenity Prayer.'"

The remarkable thing about Jim's statement is how frequently I hear it, in various forms. Even people who have no particular connection to the Lord's Prayer or the Jesus Prayer (let alone the Memorare or the Hail Mary!) or any formal prayer somehow find great consolation in the Serenity Prayer. It seems to strike a chord that transcends the boundaries of particular religious experiences to touch something intimately related to our common humanity. And remarkably, this prayer loved by so many is not generic, trite, or superficial. Quite the contrary! From the most fervent and committed believer to the most skeptical seeker, we can all find in it something of great depth and support. I pray it every day.

At various times the prayer has been attributed to the most diverse authors, from Thomas Aquinas to Cicero, from Saint Augustine to Boethius, from Marcus Aurelius to Saint Francis of Assisi. But in fact the prayer has a much more humble and recent pedigree. It was written, or at least popularized, by the twentieth-century Protestant American theologian Reinhold Niebuhr. It has taken many forms, but always comes down to three simple petitions:

Lord, grant me the serenity to accept the things I cannot change,
the courage to change the things I can,
and the wisdom to know the difference.

When I first encountered this prayer many years ago, it caught my attention, but I didn't give it much thought. It seemed a bit cliché, something you might see on a motivational poster with accompanying pictures of sprinters, pandas, sunsets, weightlifters, or waterfalls.

It took sitting in on an open Alcoholics Anonymous meeting to discover that the Serenity Prayer was much deeper than my own soul had been ready to acknowledge. In my pride and immaturity, I had mistaken simplicity for shallowness, and the universal for cliché. On a hot day in August, in the basement cafeteria of a shuttered grade school, I witnessed broken men and women pray the Serenity Prayer like I could only wish to pray it myself. Sitting on wooden chairs made for schoolchildren half their size, Christians and non-Christians alike recited from memory words they had made their own. It was prayer because it was wide open, fearless, and important dialogue with God. It was a calm cry in the darkness of their own insufficiency to a greater power to whom they had attached their will and their hopes. It was the purest and most genuine act of self-abandonment to God's will I had ever witnessed. Their prayer wasn't especially pretty, or clean; it was real, and gritty. It was the opposite of religious showmanship; it was intimate, existential, and wholly indifferent to any outsider's praise or reproach. It was prayer, plain and simple.

As I began to study and pray over the elements of the Serenity Prayer and the reasons it was so popular I realized that this simple prayer could become a major part of my own daily spiritual life.

Why? First off, its simplicity is compelling. Longer prayers can also be beautiful, and they have their place. I think of the ancient liturgical prayers, so full of theological tradition and meaning, drawing us into the mystery of God's being. But there is something endearing and eminently practical about a prayer that any of us could have composed on dozens of occasions in response to a personal dilemma. The Serenity Prayer is a trusting groan of the spirit. It is a confident cry for help.

We intuitively sense in this prayer the truth of Jesus's frequent praise of children and the need to be childlike in our own spiritual lives. We so quickly complicate things. As our minds get foggy our prayers get wordy, and then we get tired and stop praying altogether. But wasn't it Jesus, once again, who encouraged his followers to be brief in their prayers? I sincerely doubt that God is very much impressed by the elegant prose and perfect syntax of our orations if we are delivering them to look or feel smart or pious, or in the hope that the perfect set of words will magically get us what we want. Prayer consists in laying ourselves bare before him who already sees our soul's nakedness in all of its sinfulness and goodness, and who then responds by helping us take off our blinders to see ourselves and others through his eyes.

A second factor that makes the Serenity Prayer so powerful is the importance of the gift we request of God when we pray it: peace of soul, or serenity. We are asking God to replace our stress with a heart at rest. Stress can destroy our lives if we let it. We feel it in our blood when it is taking over. It starts with a little worry, which becomes anxiety, and soon enough we are enveloped in fear. In the Serenity Prayer we ask God to soak every fiber of our anxious being with his peace.

At times the thought of daily serenity feels unattainable to me. Like so many others, I have several jobs (ministries) demanding my attention, and with each passing year it feels as though my plate gets fuller. The consequences of failure become greater. More work means more responsibility, and more responsibility means more problems. With life so crowded with tasks, I would hardly describe my normal day as serene. Yet, as I am sure all of us have experienced at one time or another, with the right state of mind and with God's grace, it is possible to be peaceful even in the midst of a flurry of activity. That's the peaceful soul the Serenity Prayer seeks.

A third reason the Serenity Prayer can transform our lives is that it reminds us of another important truth: God wants us to be serene. We rightly recoil from the idea of a God who is just concerned about laying down rules and keeping us in line. This misconception of God as "cop" is especially repulsive because we know we aren't very good at keeping all the rules. In contrast, speaking to a God who wants us to have a peaceful soul—what we naturally long for—reminds us that he is on our side. That's the God saints have fallen in love with for centuries. That's the God of the Serenity Prayer. Its simple petitions point to a God who loves us, wants us to be happy, and is there to help us become our best selves.

So many people turn away from religion because, as life progresses, the demands of a relationship with God and Church seem too much to bear. Though Christianity teaches that God is love, sometimes when the Church (including me!) begins to explain what this means for us in practice, the core truth is lost or replaced by other, less important notions. We focus on what faith might demand of us if we were to go all in, rather than on the loving Father who is calling us into his embrace.

Lastly, there's another quality in the Serenity Prayer that makes it special. It is a petition for God to give us grace to do our part, rather than to bypass us and do it all on his own. That's the way it should be, a more human way. And it's generally the way God chooses to intervene in human affairs. Do you remember feeling a bit strange in school asking God to help you do well on an exam you never studied for? That's a healthy feeling because God gave us a mind and a will and we act ungratefully when we presumptuously fail to use the gifts he has already given to us with the hope that he will always bail us out. Yes, in the Serenity Prayer we are asking for the miracle of serenity in turmoil, but we are promising God at the same time that we will try to (1) accept what we cannot change, (2) act courageously to change the things we can, and (3) use our minds to distinguish between what we can change and what we cannot. That's a lot of collaboration with God's grace.

Each of the three great virtues we request in this prayer—serenity, courage, and wisdom—comes at a price. We ask for them, but we also work for them and depend on God's grace to lead us along the way. The miracle we ask for is grace to do what we would otherwise be unable to do. As powerful as we feel in the modern age, there are many aspects of our lives that make us feel strangely powerless. I meet people every day who feel trapped. For some it is their work situation (or their unemployment), for others it is their marriage or family, and still others feel imprisoned by the bad choices they have made or simply by their own inadequacies and failures. We don't need to be thrown into a barred cell to feel truly imprisoned. We can build our own prison and lock ourselves in. We allow trifling conditions to leave us feeling hopeless and empty. Isn't it amazing—and frustrating—to see how, on the one hand, science has enabled us to split atoms, map the human genome, and cure many diseases, yet on the other hand, here we remain, still held back by the defects of our own character! Does God want us to be trapped? No way! He wants to give us grace to unlock our chains and walk out of our prison.

What I most love about the Serenity Prayer is that when we learn to truly pray it—not just say it—we are obliged to put it into practice. With this prayer in our hearts, we already are learning to discern what we are able to contribute (the things we can change) and what we must simply accept and leave in God's hands (the things we cannot change). We ask for serenity, for courage, and for wisdom, and we work for them as well.

My hope is that this book will help you make this prayer a

way of life. That's what it has become for me. Of course, in my ministry I pray often and I say many prayers, and I try to make them all heartfelt. For me, however, the Serenity Prayer is different from all the rest: it is a habit, a way of life, and these are words I speak to God when I wake, before I go to sleep, when I'm nervous, when I'm grateful, when I'm confused, when I'm happy, when I fail, and when I don't know what else to say.

In each of the three parts of this book I explore one line of this wonderful prayer in depth. I use stories of people who have learned—or are in the process of learning—to find greater serenity in life. I talk about what God has done in my own life and in the lives of my family members to lead us along this three-step path. I have employed my favorite biblical stories, spiritual texts, historical facts, prayers, and meditations to help direct you along this journey toward the greater serenity, courage, and wisdom that God wants for all of us.

Before going further, I would like to make one request: would you memorize the Serenity Prayer today and pray it each day until you finish this book? That would be one simple way to tell the Holy Spirit that you are open to whatever joy-filled surprise he is waiting to give you. In this light, I have composed a very short prayer for you at the end of each chapter. Let each of these prayers be a reminder that this book is more about taking a journey of prayer and conversion than about learning something new.

PART ONE

The Serenity to Accept the Things I Cannot Change

NOT LONG AGO, my dear friend Lorie texted me somewhat in a panic. She said she was paranoid about her boss and couldn't sleep at night. "Are you afraid he is going to fire you?" I asked.

"No, I don't think so, but he is asking me to do so many things that I don't know if I can do it all, or how it's all going to turn out."

"Well, Lorie, but isn't it great that he depends so much on you? It's a sign of confidence," I responded, "and he isn't going to fire you, or get angry with you, if you can only do so much."

"I know, but this is too much, and I am not sure what to do," she said.

"But is he happy with your work production so far?"

"I'm not sure," she said, "but earlier this month he did give me a raise."

"A significant one?"

"Yes, I guess so. Twenty percent." I replied with a smiley face, saying that a lot of people would love to have that kind of unreasonable boss. For Lori, however, not even a raise and a big bonus the previous month could change how she felt now. She was oppressed by her boss's expectations. She couldn't control his requests, and she felt that things were too much for her to handle. Lorie was overwhelmed by things she felt she could not change.

In this first section of the book, we will dive into what it means to accept with serenity the things we cannot change and how we can go about doing this. Three ideas are in play: serenity, acceptance, and unchangeable realities.

At first glance, serenity might seem to be a negative concept, in the sense of referring to an absence of something—for example, the absence of agitation, of worry, of stress. If serenity were merely about the absence of certain feelings or conditions, however, we would say that being serene means being carefree—calm and unmoved by the troubles all around us. But when we meet a truly serene person, we realize that there is more to it than being carefree. Peaceful, serene people exude a sense of calm, fulfillment, and well-being. Serenity and peace of soul are positive concepts that encompass a fullness and richness of spirit that go far beyond the mere absence of something bad. A person cannot be truly serene if she is empty inside, even if no problems are pressing down on her. The serenity we pray for is holistic—it encompasses all of who we are. This serenity is related to a deep-seated confidence that all the important things in our life are okay, or they are going to be okay, because God is on our side and knows what he permits and why he does so.

The serene soul rests in the certainty of being loved and cared for by the perfect lover—God himself.

If serenity is a state of being, the second element in play, acceptance, is an action. In Latin the word is *accipere,* meaning to take something to oneself, to make it one's own. When we accept gifts offered by others, we receive them gratefully as items coming into our possession. Our acceptance of gifts is the opposite of rejection, the unwillingness to take to ourselves what is offered. Acceptance, in this context, also implies a certain amount of consent, such as when we accept an apology or a proposal. Notice that acceptance goes well beyond mere resignation. To accept a person into one's home or circle of friends involves a welcoming disposition, and to accept an idea means to embrace it, assimilate it, and identify with it. In our prayer, we ask specifically for the serenity that comes from this sort of welcoming attitude toward the difficult realities in our lives that we cannot change.

What are those realities that are beyond our power to alter? What are the unchangeable realities in our life that we are asking God to help us accept? There are too many to enumerate, but it may be helpful to form an idea of some of the ones that are hardest for us to accept. We can start, of course, with our past, our personal history. All that is written is written. The "hand we were dealt"—parents, siblings, education, talents (or lack thereof), traumas and tragedies, our good and bad choices and their consequences—all of this is, in one sense, water under the bridge. These are the things that don't change, no matter what we wish or do. We can rebel against them or embrace their reality. We can learn from them or allow them to condition us. They simply are, because they were. Few people are completely satisfied with their lives. Few people love everything about themselves—and most people who do aren't awfully fun to be around!

In this first part of the book, we will bring these three concepts home. We seek serenity, and we acknowledge that we cannot find it unless we are willing to accept certain things, because resisting unchangeable realities is not only unproductive but actually destructive. This first petition of the Serenity Prayer requires a certain discipline to take the steps necessary to shape our fundamental dispositions in a constructive way, and it also requires a willingness to trust. We ask, believing that we will receive. We seek, with every confidence that we will find. We knock, with the assurance that the door will be opened to us.

CHAPTER 1

A Peace That Comes from God

❧

IT HAS BECOME a cliché that the safest thing to wish or pray for out loud without offending anyone is world peace, which is now a staple of Miss America pageants, high school graduations, and humanitarian luncheons. And while there is much to be said in its favor, world peace is sometimes a place-holder for the naive wish, "Can't we all just get along?" That wish is naive because it suggests that peace can be achieved through behavior or policy instead of conversion of heart. In our quest for "world peace," we look outward to avoid having to look inward. As the great bishop Fulton Sheen once wrote: "World wars are only projections of the conflicts waged inside the souls of modern men, for nothing happens in the external world that has not first happened within a soul."[1] This is true. What we really want, even more than world peace, is peace of soul. Peace within.

When we pray for the serenity to accept the things we can-not change, we are asking for this profound peace. It is a deeper, more lasting peace that does not depend on things going our way, but rather on our willingness to allow God to order things in his way and with his timing.

Jesus came as the Prince of Peace, and he promised his disciples the gift of a peace that the world cannot give (John 14:27). This peace is more than mere "getting along" or the absence of armed conflict. Jesus meant something deeper, more durable. Peace in this world is always precarious, always threatened. We can have it for a while, only to be robbed of it again. Just as the surface of the ocean can be calm for a while, then erupt into violent swells, so our peace seems always at risk of falling apart. Even those who have everything going for them—health, relationships, wealth—must live with the knowledge that at any moment these things can be taken away.

Allowing God to order things in his way and in his time is hard because it means letting go of things we want to hold on to. And letting go of things that really do need fixing can feel like injustice, irresponsibility, or indifference on our part. Sometimes I have even felt guilty about trying to leave in God's hands the things I know I cannot change, as if worrying about them means I'm doing something positive about them. But that's shallow thinking on my part. Serenity of soul is not equal to being in control. Far below the surface of the ocean lie depths that are undisturbed by the fierce storms that rage above. Where we see only choppy waves God sees the potential for calm and the path to peace and order.

Have you noticed how easy it is to hand over the steering wheel of your life when the waters are calm? It is easy to trust God when we have already engineered the outcome we want. It isn't so easy—but this is what we request in our prayer—to tell God we will no longer fight for absolute control because we trust his control is best.

Peace does not begin with nations, or even among family

members or friends. It begins with our own humble relationship with God. It begins when we pray, "God, grant me your peace, in your way, in your time."

One of the most beautiful and profound books I have ever read is a slim volume written by the Jesuit priest Jean-Pierre de Caussade back in the early 1700s. Called *Abandonment to Divine Providence,* it lays out a simple path to deep interior peace through loving acceptance of God's will in every moment. God is ever active, de Caussade writes, in the "sacrament of the present moment," and our surrender to him is a path to both holiness and peace.[2] We, like Saint Paul before his conversion, are often "kicking against the goads" (Acts 26:14), resisting God's plan for us, and this brings us stress and anxiety. Worrying, because we fail to trust, we are left restless and agitated.

A serenity to accept the things we cannot change means much more than simple resignation before our powerlessness to alter our situation. It means embracing both the pleasant and the unpleasant realities of our life as the backdrop against which we, with God's assistance, are working out the drama of our existence. This backdrop has been willed or permitted by God and is perfectly suited to his plan for our ultimate joy. It includes many things that we have no power to change—our history, our education, our upbringing, our family, our physique, our temperament and inclinations. So many things about each of us are simply givens, but they are givens that we are not merely to tolerate but to rejoice in! The particulars of our backdrops are not fatal flaws, but precious tools to use in our fulfillment and the mission God has called us to.

The greatest roadblock to our peace of soul often stems from our unwillingness to truly accept the things we cannot change. We dislike them. They frustrate us. Our inability to change our situation angers us and keeps us from peace. For this reason, even as we pray for serenity, we are also praying for the grace to truly embrace the things we cannot change, to see them as part of God's plan for us and a revelation of his love. They are not simply bad luck, and they are not an insurmountable barrier to our happiness or personal fulfillment. In fact, having already happened, they are a necessary part of our fulfillment.

I know a young, single woman who has no surviving relatives. Rebecca's mother committed suicide, her father died young (she was obliged to take him off life support), and finally her only grandmother—who had been more like a mother to her—died too. Rebecca always reminds me that while her relatively new faith in God and in heaven is a deep source of comfort for her, her life is still marked by pain and loneliness. Embracing God's plan doesn't mean freedom from suffering. Recently, Rebecca wrote this to me:

> *Acceptance is not usually passive. It can be, but it is usually based on action. It is an active decision to trust and love God more and accept his will, in spite of all. Also, to show love and serve others. I'm not there yet, in this last regard. This morning's passage from Oswald Chambers' devotional helped me. He said that suffering often removes a person's shallowness but doesn't always make a person better. Through divorcing ourselves from disordered attachment to self, we can become "nourishment" for others.*

What's impressive about Rebecca's spiritual journey is her active pursuit of understanding and loving God's will for her, even when she feels so much pain. Her daily reading of a devotional and her attempts to "show love and serve others" are just two examples of a persistent commitment to the goal of accepting—indeed, embracing—the things she cannot change.

The great German theologian Karl Adam once wrote that "reality is the expression of the Father's Will."[3] Isn't that consoling? God's will—the good he does and even the evil he permits in this fallen world—is never for our destruction, but always for our good! Remember the words of Jeremiah: "For surely I know the plans I have for you, says the Lord, plans for your welfare and not for harm, to give you a future with hope" (Jeremiah 29:11).

In a television program I once saw, an artist would invite small children to come up and scribble on his canvas. The challenge was for him to produce something artistic and beautiful out of something deeply flawed. I was astonished at how he was able to do this. He would step back, examine the scribble, and then start drawing with it, incorporating it into a new and bigger idea. Suddenly what had seemed senseless and random became part of a beautiful piece of art. I think this is what God does with our disorders and failings, when we allow Him. Like the television artist, he doesn't erase our scribbling—our sins—and start over from scratch. He integrates them into a new work of art, one better than we could possibly have imagined.

∞

Lord, please grant me today a taste of your peace, a peace the world cannot give. Help me to embrace my past instead of wishing for another, and to look for your action today in the sacrament of the moment.

CHAPTER 2

Safe from All Distress

❧

IN THE liturgical celebration of the Lord's Supper, after the Our Father prayer, we pray that God will "deliver us from every evil and grant us his peace in our day" so that we may be "safe from all distress." In God's eyes too, distress and anxiety are enemies of our soul. They are obstacles to our ability to live in his peace, in our day, accepting the things we cannot change.

Jesus tells his disciples not to worry about all the things that nonbelievers might fret about. He tells them not to stress over their food or clothing, and not to panic over tomorrow's concerns when today's are sufficient. He is telling them and us that life can be simpler than we make it out to be. He then invites us to prioritize our concerns, saying, "Seek first the Kingdom," and promising that if we do so everything else will work itself out (Matthew 6:25–34). Jesus is telling us that, in fact, there is no need to worry—we can rest peacefully in the truth that things we cannot change are under his care.

Good Saint Martha, the sister of Lazarus and Mary of Bethany, is the consummate hostess (Luke 10:38–41). When the

Lord comes to her house, she runs about trying to make every-thing perfect for him, making every sacrifice in order to do so. But her hyper-concern about hosting the perfect party puts her nerves on edge and, ironically, ends up causing her to be rude to her esteemed guest. Frustrated that her sister Mary has left her to do all the work while she sits at the master's feet and enjoys his company, Martha marches over to Jesus and demands that he tell Mary to help her. Knowing Martha's good heart, Jesus chides Martha gently. "Martha, Martha," he says, "you worry and fret over many things. Few are needed, indeed only one."

Jesus is not counseling irresponsibility. He isn't suggesting that we show up for work only when we feel like it, or fail to plan our family budget. Nothing in the Gospel depicts Jesus as a hakuna matata flower child with a carefree, devil-may-care atti-tude. Jesus simply invites us to reprioritize our concerns and to realize that most of what troubles us really doesn't deserve so much of our emotional energy and that what really does matter could use more of it.

What distresses me the most and robs me of peace of soul? Is it really as important as I make it out to be? Most of the things that seem to be emergencies in the moment are forgot-ten within a few days, and sometimes even within a few hours. Whatever had me in a tizzy last week is now forgotten, buried like a city in the desert under the sands of time. Something that seems so dire to me in one moment can be blotted from my memory a short time later.

An important step in the spiritual exercise of overcoming distress or anxiety is choosing to trust that you are not alone, and then to move forward with that knowledge. If everything depends on you, that is a terribly heavy burden to bear. If your future and the future of your family rest solely on your strength and personal qualities, how can you hope to succeed? But does it *all* really depend on you? Absolutely not. The old adage "do your best and forget about the rest," properly understood, is true. Why worry about what you cannot change? But the adage is even truer when doing your best includes giving over to God the cause of your distress and allowing him to take care of the rest. Just as in a business venture in which there are minor and major partners and the major partner has ultimate responsibility and power, so it is in the Christian life. When we have done all that we can, we can forget about the rest because we know our Major Partner in the business of life—the Holy Spirit—has things under control.

The lyrics of the song "I Offer My Life" by songwriters Don Moen and Claire Cloninger express beautifully the giving over of our anxiety to the Lord.

> *All that I am, all that I have*
> *I lay them down before You, oh Lord*
> *All my regrets, all my acclaims*
> *The joy and the pain, I'm making them Yours*
>
> *Lord, I offer my life to You*
> *Everything I've been through, use it for Your glory*
> *Lord, I offer my days to You*
> *Lifting my praise to You as a pleasing sacrifice*
> *Lord, I offer you my life*[1]

The great saints of the Bible knew how to do this. Saint Peter invites us to place our cares on Jesus's shoulders and trust in him: "Unload all your burden on to him, since he is concerned about you" (1 Peter 5:7). That is profoundly consoling.

But should we really put all of this on God? Shouldn't we ask God for permission before we throw all of this on him? We do have his permission. In fact, this is what he begs us to do.

"Come to me, all you that are weary and are carrying heavy burdens," Jesus tells us, "and I will give you rest" (Matthew 11:28). I don't know whether there are more consoling words than these anywhere in the Bible. They tell us that Jesus understands that we are burdened and anxious and that he is sympathetic. He wants to assist us, and he invites us to turn to him. He continues: "Take my yoke upon you, and learn from me; for I am gentle and humble in heart, and you will find rest for your souls. For my yoke is easy, and my burden is light" (Matthew 11:29–30). In a way, it seems that Jesus is asking us to swap our burden for his. He wants to take on our loads and offers us in exchange the sweet yoke of following him.

∞

All that I am, all that I have
I lay them down before You, oh Lord
All my regrets, all my acclaims
The joy and the pain, I'm making them Yours

CHAPTER 3

Work as if Everything Depends on You, and Pray as if Everything Depends on God

❧

C HOOSING TO turn over to God our cares and worries about the things we cannot change will not make us passive. In fact, it will make us more effective. Our minds become clearer to act wisely and to do what we know we can and should do.

Do you remember Aesop's fables? Aesop was a Phrygian who lived in the sixth century BC. Although he obviously didn't have the advantage of having heard Jesus's life and message, the moralizing fables attributed to him are filled with fundamental truths about the human condition, including the value of hard work and responsible living. In his fable "The Ant and the Grasshopper," Aesop told of a very industrious little ant who spends his summer hauling food into his anthill, storing up for the long winter. Every day he trudges past a grasshopper who devotes his summer days to playing his fiddle and ridiculing the hardworking ant for his foolishness. Indeed, as long as summer lasts, it seems like the grasshopper is the wiser of the two, living out his days eating, drinking, and making merry, while the poor ant slaves away.

But, as you will recall, eventually winter arrives, and things change—radically. Now the ant has the upper hand, enjoying the fruits of his labors. The cold and hungry grasshopper is reduced to begging, while the ant rests cozy and well fed in his anthill.

The serenity we seek is not born of irresponsibility. It is not by ignoring our duties that we find peace of soul. We have all known people who, like the grasshopper in the story, don't know how to live responsibly, or simply won't. They run up credit card debts with no means of paying them off, or they live off other people's generosity because they haven't bothered to save up for themselves.

We are right to recoil from the idea that serenity is compatible with—or even worse, the fruit of—indifference to the way things should be. But neither does serenity reside in the reverse—feeling guilty that we are not depending on God if we do work hard and go after our goals. The virtue here lies in the middle: setting good goals and going after them with gusto and without living as if everything depends on us or fretting constantly about the future.

Another adage comes immediately to mind in this regard. It is a much older "sister proverb" to the Serenity Prayer and is attributed to the founder of the Jesuits, the Spaniard Ignatius of Loyola. He counseled: "Work as if everything depended on you, and pray as if everything depended on God." When working, then, we do so knowing how important a part we play. Yet when praying, we call to mind that without God, not even our work will save us. Our prayer is a necessary counterbalance to our action and reminds us who is ultimately in charge. As Jesus rhetorically asks us, "Can any of you by worrying add a single hour to your span of life?" (Matthew 6:27). In other words, we are called to plan, to save, and to work, all the time knowing that we are in his hands. God asks of us fidelity, not success.

The serenity we seek arises partly from knowing that we have done all we can and the rest is up to God. There is a true peace of soul that comes over us when we have put forth our best effort. Like a farmer who has tilled his field and sown his seed and now sits back to wait for the crops to grow, when we have done our part we can rest with the assurance that the fruits of our labors ultimately depend on God. The Christian life can be conceived as a collaborative effort, a limited partnership, or even a joint venture, with God always the major business partner who works alongside us and makes up for our deficiencies.

I'm a golfer. Maybe that's putting it too strongly—I like to play golf. Besides the thrill that comes with trying to make a little white ball go into a hole in the ground several hundred yards away from the tee (I know, it sounds a bit crazy), I love golf because it is for me a spiritual experience in more than one respect. When I see a beautifully designed course or a magnificent natural landscape, I connect with the grandeur of God. And on the rare occasion when I hit a good shot, I get excited to see how I can train my mind and body to do what they should and I begin to think that someday I might become a decent golfer. Admittedly, that fond hope might just barely qualify as spiritual, but there's more. Golf, like no other sport, allows for important conversations, in a relaxed environment, with people you might not otherwise talk with for such an extended period of time.

During a writing retreat near Lake Tahoe, I was invited to deal with my writer's block by playing at a magnificent new course called Clear Creek Tahoe. It is an unknown gem that

I'm sure will soon be discovered by golf experts as a world-class course. Every hole is uniquely and artistically pulled out of the natural contour of the Nevada side of the Sierras. After the first hole, I knew that for the next three hours I was going to be in a little piece of heaven. What I didn't know then was that I would also be moved spiritually by both the conversation with my host and his technical golf advice.

I had never met Colin before, but I was immediately taken by his natural goodness and his talent as a teaching professional. Since he knew I was a priest, the conversation eventually turned to religion, as it almost always does. He asked me about how I decided to become a priest. When he then asked me if my parents were priests too, I knew he wasn't Catholic, but I could sense an eagerness to know more about God and faith. He later told me that he was not raised with any religion, but that as a child he had always been fascinated by prayer and that going into churches brought him peace. One topic led to another, and soon, at his prodding, we were engaged in a deep conversation about mortality, heaven, God, prayer, faith and reason, and life's meaning. Granted, I wouldn't have planned or even encouraged such a heady conversation on a golf course, but Colin's humility, sincerity, openness, and sharp intelligence had the conversation flowing effortlessly, and I'm sure I learned at least as much from him as he said he did from me.

I believe it was on the 590-yard 13th hole, ironically named "Contemplation," that Colin related a golf technique to the way we should live life. He started out by commenting on my swing. "It's all about tempo. When all else fails, just remember: tempo, tempo, tempo." In golf lingo that means, slow down your swing and let the club do the work for you. "Remember," he said, "there's a reason we call it a 'swing' and not a 'hit.'" He continued: "In golf, we have fourteen clubs in our bag, but we only need one swing. If you slow it down and get yourself out of the way of the club, the rest will take care of itself." Then he looked up and said, with a broad smile, "I guess that's a little bit like life."

Colin is so right. When we try to force our will, when we try to speed up the process, when we fail to get out of the way, when we act one way one day and another way the next, that's when things go wrong. On the other hand, when we are confident in our standing before God and others, when our major aspiration is to get to heaven and bring as many people as possible with us, then life is quite simple. This simplicity allows us to confront with greater ease whatever comes our way. A committed Christian facing shame or fame, triumph or defeat, sickness or health, financial crisis or wealth, doesn't have his life turned upside down, because these experiences don't change him and his major aspiration remains within reach.

Whether by personality we tend to be more like Aesop's ant (maybe a bit of a worrier?) or his grasshopper (definitely irresponsible), we can change. We can choose to work as if everything depends on us and to pray as if everything depends on God. Working and praying this way will bring us a long way down the road to accepting the things we cannot change.

∞

Dear Lord, today I will try to collaborate with your plan for me by doing the best I can in everything I do. Grateful for life and time, I will work hard according to priorities, and at the same time, because I am confident that you are in control, I will try to focus more on treating people with kindness and respect than on my agenda items.

CHAPTER 4

Patience Leads to Peace

❧

AN OLD POEM on patience attributed to John Dewey goes like this:

> *Patience is a virtue,*
> *Possess it if you can,*
> *Seldom found in woman,*
> *Never found in man.*

Of course, like most generalizations, this one isn't quite true, but it does express in a catchy way the reality that patience is as rare as it is good. And it is good because it is a precursor to serenity.

When we think of patience, we usually think of the ability not to give up and to wait for the right moment, but patience means much more than that. Patience (from the Latin *patior,* "to suffer"!) really means the ability to bear with hardship. I rather like the definition offered by Dictionary.com: "the bearing of provocation, annoyance, misfortune, or pain, without complaint, loss of temper, irritation, or the like." That sums it up quite well.

Seen this way, we can understand why patience is such an important virtue if we wish to achieve genuine peace of soul. Bad, tough things will always happen to us, but if every bad thing puts us out of sorts, then we are at the mercy of fortune, going up and down with our lot in life. If our peace of soul can be stolen from us as soon as someone cuts us off on the highway, what kind of peace is that? If we are happy when things go well and bad-tempered when they don't, we will never find true and lasting serenity.

This is certainly true of the big things that can go wrong in life, but it's true of the little things as well. Off the top of my head, I can think of a few unimportant things that bug me more than they should. I don't like long meetings. I don't like long phone calls. I really don't like the slightest hint of passive-aggressive modes of operating. If I gave myself some time to think about it I could come up with a few more. But guess what? I have no doubt that other people are annoyed by my tendency to shirk long meetings and phone calls and the way I respond to passive-aggressive behavior.

If we choose to focus on things that bother us, we will never be at peace. We will be at the mercy of those around us. The serenity to accept the things we cannot change must involve the ability to be patient with these things and decide that they will not alter our state of mind and heart. During long meetings I pray, "Jesus, grant me a tiny portion of the patience you have daily toward me."

Given the fact that we cannot avoid all trouble in life, we have a choice to make regarding how we will deal with what comes our way. We can live in bitterness and sorrow, either from the real and present woes that afflict us or from the fear that trouble could be just around the corner. Or we can choose to live in peace despite our real trials and tribulations and in the confidence that nothing can befall us that we cannot handle with God's grace.

When we talk about the serenity to accept the things we cannot change, we are obviously referring especially to the negative things we cannot change, and we are also speaking about patience—about our capacity to live in enduring peace in spite of the negative aspects of our lives that we would change if we could.

Even if you are no biblical scholar, you are probably familiar with Saint Paul's famous "Hymn to Charity" in the thirteenth chapter of his first letter to the Corinthians. Anyone who has attended Christian weddings has heard it read as an exhortation to couples to begin their married lives in true love for one another. Paul lists a number of qualities of love: "Love is kind," he says. "Love is not envious or boastful or arrogant or rude," he adds. And so on: "Love does not insist on its own way; it is not irritable or resentful; it does not rejoice in wrongdoing, but rejoices in the truth." But of all these wonderful qualities, the one that heads the list is patience. "Love is patient," Paul begins. We can never really love, in fact, if we are unable to bear with another person's faults and deficiencies. Love that is not patient is not true love. And how can we possibly be truly serene if we are incapable of loving?

If love is patient and God is love, it follows that God is patient. This lesson was taught to me by a gentleman at one of my previous parishes. Scott and his wife were going through terrible times when he came to me for spiritual advice. Shortly after they were married, Scott came to see that his wife's control and anger issues were much more serious than he had previously thought. While they were dating, he had seen glimpses of what he thought might be a problem, but it was nothing like what he was witnessing now. What used to be rational disagreements were now screaming fits that would sometimes turn physical. Throughout the workday Jill would send countless urgent texts meant to reengage Scott in their most recent fight. By the time Scott came to me, he was a broken man. He was embarrassed that his new marriage was breaking down so quickly. He felt like a lousy husband, and he feared for his newborn daughter and the psychological impact on her of growing up in an angry household.

After a couple of sessions of spiritual work, I recommended to Scott that he and Jill see a family therapist. As Scott predicted, Jill refused to go. Three months later, however, when Scott moved into a hotel to escape the violent home environment, Jill agreed to go once to a counselor. That visit eventually led to Jill being diagnosed with bipolar disorder. When Scott came to tell me this, he was smiling from ear to ear. I was sure there had been a major breakthrough. Why else would he be so happy? But in fact, things weren't better. Jill rejected the doctor's diagnosis and refused to be treated in any way. This sounded like terrible news to me, but Scott saw it very differently. "My wife is sick," he said. "The woman I married and love is in need of a doctor. The reason why she doesn't want to follow the doctor's orders is because her sickness makes her think she is not sick. That's not her fault; it just means I have to work harder at getting her better without her help."

Six months later, Scott came to see me. When I asked him how he was, he replied that he was doing great.

"And Jill?"

"She is still very sick, and still doesn't want help. But I think she is getting to the point where she might agree to go back to the counselor or the doctor." That didn't sound very good to me. In many ways, things had become worse for Scott. Jill had more reason to think that he was out to get her now that he and the doctor agreed that she needed help. She had more reasons to be angry. But I will never forget the spiritual maturity Scott expressed in that meeting. He was still broken, but he was no longer in despair. "How are you getting along?" I asked him. "Are you okay?"

"Surprisingly, I really am doing well," he said. "The first turning point for me was when I realized Jill was sick. But the big moment came when I was sitting alone in the church on my way back from work. I was trying to get the strength to go home and face Jill. I don't know what it was. It wasn't a voice from heaven or anything, but all of a sudden I thought of how patient God has been with me over the course of my life. All of a sudden, I saw myself through God's eyes, as the sick patient in need of patience. When I went home that day, I gave Jill a hug for the first time in many months. And every day since then I have tried to do one special thing, one loving surprise for her each and every day. Sometimes she takes it the wrong way. But deep down I know why I am doing it. As a follower of Jesus, who has carried the burden of my sin, I am called to carry patiently the burden of the one I love."

Patience also means the ability to wait. One of the hardships that patience bears is how slowly some things come about. Patience is a biblical virtue in this sense as well. Throughout the Psalms we are told to hold fast in attending the Lord's coming. Psalm 27:14, for instance, urges: "Wait for the Lord, take courage; be stouthearted, wait for the Lord!" Waiting requires courage; it requires "stoutheartedness" (what a great word)! If we will not wait, we will not receive the many blessings the Lord intends for us. The Lord is not a God of quick fixes and fifteen-minute spiritual oil-changes, but a God of long-term and indeed eternal promises. So our patience is exercised not only with one another but also with God himself! In the end, it is in waiting for the Lord that we learn to trust him, for he responds over time.

The good news is that patience is a virtue that is richly rewarded. God *is* faithful. He is true to his promises.

∞

Lord, I am not very good at patience. But today I will bear with faith and love whatever burden you allow, out of love for you and love for those around me. Grant me the grace to wait with expectant hope, because I know that you will be faithful to your promises.

CHAPTER 5

God Never Leaves Us Alone

❧

WHEN WE talk about accepting the things we cannot change, we acknowledge our powerlessness before many of the realities of our existence. We can't get taller (the rack never really worked), we can't get smarter (though watching less TV would probably help), we can't get younger (no matter how many hours we spend at the gym), and we can't get much prettier (those attempts usually backfire). But this is just the beginning. If we were to make a list of the things in life we cannot change, it would be miles long. We can't solve world hunger, we can't fix the federal deficit, we can't cure cancer, and we can't change other people. When it comes down to it, the list of what we *cannot* change simply overwhelms those very few things we *can* change.

Reflecting on the imbalance between what we can change and what we can't change would be rather depressing if we didn't also meditate on God's presence and action in our lives and in the world. God can change all of these things, if he so wills, and if he doesn't will it, then we don't need to worry. We have this confidence because God tells us over and over again in the sacred scriptures that he is with us, that he cares for us, and that he will provide all that we need. In Psalm 23, the psalmist prays: "Even were I to walk in a ravine as dark as death, I should fear no danger, for you are at my side."

Living with faith in God's constant presence builds context for facing the reality of our limitations. We are brought up to believe that we are free. We live in a free country, have free will, and go about as we please, free from restraint. Yet honesty compels us to acknowledge the real limits on our freedom. There are so many things we simply cannot do. Sometimes we are limited by logical impossibilities (like not being able to make a square circle); other times our limitations are physical, and sometimes they are intellectual or moral.

Accepting the things we cannot change begins with recognizing this imperfect reality. Before we get to serenity, courage, and wisdom, we have to face the facts. There are things in our life that aren't right. Few people really love their jobs. Marriage, even a good one, is often more difficult than we would have imagined on our wedding day. And our vices and habits, all those things that keep us from being better people, and more successful people, are real and present. As life goes on, these realities force us to revise the dreams and expectations of our youth.

Our imperfections and limitations can lead us to adopt a jaded worldview as our ideals shrink and reality seems more and more of a drudgery. But this doesn't need to happen—deeper self-knowledge and acceptance can lead us instead toward deeper faith.

The limits to our freedom imposed by our present reality don't have to lessen our dignity as persons. They can ennoble us. Our weakness allows us to need others and to take our place before God in the truth of our dependence on him. Over the course of our lives the "rugged individualism" that we idolize turns out to be something of a sham. Part of being human is being frail. Essentially, we are far frailer than we like to admit.

If we have yet to turn our lives over to God completely, our fragility is good reason to be fearful. But when we learn to pray as Jesus taught us ("thy kingdom come, thy will be done, on earth as it is in heaven"), our fragility becomes our strength. We are strong enough to pray for God's intervention. We are strong enough to admit that we are weak. We are strong enough to cry out to God as needy children. We are strong enough to pray for God's will to be done, no matter what that is. This is the spiritual genius of Saint Paul's shocking claim, "When I am weak, then I am strong" (2 Corinthians 12:10).

The next words of the Our Father require even more humility: "Give us this day our daily bread. . . ." Jesus doesn't tell us to pray for retirement security. He doesn't tell us to pray for wealth. He doesn't tell us to pray for final solutions. Instead, he tells us to ask him for whatever we need for today! The God of the universe, who could provide for every imaginable need, wants me to be fed by him one day at a time!

Since God, by definition, is perfect and does not need us, his desire for us to live through him, day by day, must be for our own good. I have witnessed many average people become very holy souls, and happy souls, precisely through the experience of becoming dependent on "daily bread" from Jesus. My Uncle Dexter was for many years an architect in a big firm in New York City. A self-described workaholic, Dex worked long days and most weekends and gave 100 percent of himself to the success of the firm. As a result of the financial crisis of 2008, new construction in New York slowed considerably and Dex's firm was forced to downsize and eventually close its doors. Now in his early sixties, Dex found himself unemployed and in a job market that prized young professionals willing to work for nothing. Uncle Dex searched for a new position for over a year with no luck. He and his wife, my aunt Mary Ellen, reluctantly made the choice to leave the city and go to Texas to look for new opportunities. It was a stinging personal and professional blow.

Almost immediately upon arriving in Austin, Uncle Dex became very sick. He was losing a lot of weight and had no energy. He was in great pain. Month after month, and then year after year, my aunt and uncle sojourned through every doctor's office, hospital, and procedure that might offer them a clear diagnosis. But to this day they haven't found a clear answer. Dex still lives with more pain than any of us have ever known.

What most people don't know is that during his last year in New York City and the first months in Austin, God was working overtime on Dex's soul, and Dex was cooperating. Without anyone knowing, Dex began to go back to church and entered into adult religious education. He kept this faith journey quiet as he discreetly opened his soul to God.

I did not become aware of both the seriousness of Uncle Dex's health struggles and the intensity of his spiritual journey until I stayed with them for a few days in Austin. It was then that I heard Mary Ellen and Dex first talk about how praying for "daily bread"—grace from God for the present moment— had transformed their lives. This is how Dex later described it to me in a letter.

Hi Jonathan,

I think I mentioned to you the many times I found myself sitting inside St. Ignatius Church on my way to Central Park in our last year in New York: not expecting or wanting anything. I think it was then that I received the gift of knowing that whatever happens, God's love for me, and my love for Him would ensure without question that each day is complete and full with everything I could ever wish for. It was a beautiful, and timely, gift, given in the house of God I knew I belonged in.

I had this gift reaffirmed in my heart when I was later confirmed into the Church.

At about the same time as my personal visits to that church, a priest there who knew we were going to leave New York, with the anxiety of not knowing if I would find a job soon, talked to Mary Ellen and me about making plans. He reminded us that planning ahead is good . . . but not too far ahead. It is our daily life together loving each other, loving God, and loving our neighbors that will keep the daily bread fresh and nourishing. Plan too far ahead . . . and the bread gets stale: ". . . you know," he said, "like the manna that has fallen to the ground and lays there and rots!" And he laughed.

We will never forget his loving sendoff.

There was more to Uncle Dex's letter, but before you read on, do you see how God was working behind the scenes in his life? Dex's objective was good, and it was urgent: to find a new job. But God's objective for him was much bigger and even more important: to give Dex the lasting peace he was seeking through a personal relationship with himself. God was also getting Dex ready for a much bigger challenge that Dex would soon have to confront.

Then came my unexpected sickness. Its tedious healing process—and the side issues that still require attention— have given me (and Mary Ellen) an even fuller sense of the message from our priest friend in New York to "... Give us this day our daily bread."

I saw how worried my family and friends were ... how they saw me sick as they had never seen me before. My son Matt said, "Dad, this just isn't like you. You've never been sick." And I could see his disbelief and feel his fear and confusion.

Mary Ellen's love for me and her determination to get me well brought us even closer to each other.

But with each member of my family and some friends— concerned, confused, loving, supportive—I saw the suffering that my own sickness was causing them.

I tried to show progress. Every Sunday morning I made all adult religious education meetings preparing for Confirmation; all birthdays were celebrated; Mother's Days, Father's Days, other special days were made happy occasions; barbeques and swimming afternoons brought us all together for happy times.

But the concern and suffering of the family, the seemingly inconsequential moments of awkwardness that are just a part of trying to connect with the pain and suffering of a loved one, the loss of the comfortable feeling of daily routine and steadiness in the family, were there. And I worried even more about the effect my sickness was having on others close to me.

But in the midst of this very significant new challenge, at the end of each day—not knowing at the day's beginning where it would come from or what it would be—Mary Ellen and I would thank God for His great gift of that day's daily bread ... unexpected grace or blessing, inexplicable strength, support.

The "gift"—it was invisible and immeasurable. But . . . the gift was in our hearts . . . its protective power received in the church . . . its presence . . . always there as much as God's love is always there.

Dex's big grace was to have learned experientially that God never leaves us alone, and that if he allows it he gives us all that we need to not only get through it but even to become better for it.

God plays a much bigger part in our lives than we will ever know. He is active even when we can't see him. Jesus likens this action of the Holy Spirit to the wind (John 3:8): we can't see it; we can only experience its effects. Pope Benedict XVI once wrote that "God is not the prisoner of his own eternity, not limited to the solely spiritual; . . . he is capable of operating here and now, in the midst of my world."[1] As far away as he may sometimes seem, he is actually closer than we could imagine. He is our rock and our fortress. The more we rely on him the more peaceful we become.

So our inability to change certain things does not signify idle resignation, or fatality, or defeatism, but rather a bracing realism. We accept the adventure of human life the way it is, in all its splendor and mystery. It also challenges us to grow in our confidence in God. He will change what he wants to change, and we must simply work with the rest the way it is, knowing that we are not alone.

The original twelve-step program developed for Alcoholics Anonymous drives home the principle of serene acceptance of what we are powerless to change, together with a confident turning to God. The first step requires a frank admittance of our utter powerlessness, and specifically (in the case of AA) a powerlessness to overcome alcoholism. In the second step, we recognize a "Higher Power," a power "greater than ourselves," who alone can solve the problem. And the third step involves "a decision to turn our will and our lives over to the care of God as we understand Him."

Whether we suffer from addiction or not, admitting that we are powerless over many things is a giant step toward inner peace, for it leads us to lean confidently on the true Power that can change all things.

At the heart of this spiritual lesson is the truth that God is real and supremely good. We begin the Serenity Prayer not by turning inward on ourselves, but by turning outward, addressing God as "Lord." Recognizing our need, we ask him: "Lord, grant me. . . ." We are acting from faith in God's existence, in his ability to help, and in his promise that he will act.

∞

Lord, I thank you for those things in my life that reveal to me my need of you. I entrust to your care not only my hopes and desires, but also my frailty and sin. Take, Lord, receive, all that I am and want to be. Today I will remind myself that you have not left me alone, and that you will always be by my side.

CHAPTER 6

If God Can Change It, Why Doesn't He?

❧

PRAYING DEEPLY for serenity to accept the things I cannot change is nearly impossible if at some level I am still blaming God for not changing these things for me. The temptation to distrust, blame, or resent God's ways is wholly human. If I were God, I would do things differently. I think I would eliminate hunger, and floods, and earthquakes. I would have thought twice before creating some people who have made so many others suffer. Certainly mosquitoes could disappear without anybody really missing them. I would change a few things about myself too, airbrushing out a few needless moral and physical blemishes.

Most of us have good ideas about how the world could be made into a better place. So why doesn't God do it? How to improve things seems so very clear to us. Doesn't he get it? Doesn't he care as much as we do about little children who suffer? About poor people who go to bed hungry at night? About people with no jobs?

I have to believe that he does care. In fact, I believe that he cares much, much more than I do. At the same time, he cares so much about us that he is willing to allow our free will to have real consequences. We live in a fallen world because our first parents rejected God and his order for creation in the Garden of Eden. They wanted it their way, and God respected their wish. We want it our way, and God respects that too.

Imagine, on the contrary, if every time we tried to do evil, God were to intervene and protect us and others from all harm. We would be glorified robots. Free will exercised without consequences is fiction.

God was willing to risk the presence of all the evil in this world for the chance of entering into a relationship of love with us. For God, every act of human love is that precious.

God's love for us goes even further. Although we have sinned and chosen to do things our way, God makes a promise to us that out of every instance of suffering and sin in this world, he will bring out of it a good even greater than the good that has been lost and that we now mourn. We see the fulfillment of this promise most perfectly in the person of Jesus Christ, who gave up his life so that we might live with him forever in eternity, where every tear will be wiped away.

For this reason, we can have confidence that God knows what he is doing. If he doesn't do things my way, I'm the one with poor, shortsighted vision, not him. Someday we will all find out how everything had a purpose and came together in a wonderful symphony of God's goodness. Some people would call this pie-in-the-sky optimism, or a Pollyanna-ish, fairy-tale faith. I don't think that's what it is. My confidence that God knows what he is doing comes not only from the history of God's dealings with his people, as we read in the Bible, but also from my own experience with God's goodness in my life.

When we don't understand why things are going the way they are, there is good reason to give God the benefit of the doubt.

There are many mysteries in life, and there is perhaps none as troubling as the mystery of evil. In his last published book before his death, *Memory and Identity,* St. John Paul II devoted the first six chapters to what he called the *mysterium iniquitatis*—the mystery of evil. It has been a stumbling block for philosophers and common people alike since the beginning of time. It is so hard to understand how a God who is all-good and all-powerful allows bad things to happen in the world. Some of it can be explained as simply God's respect for human freedom (since much suffering results from people's bad choices), but much of it cannot be explained this way. What about earthquakes and floods? Little children with horrible birth defects? Terrible diseases and calamities?

There can be only one satisfying explanation for all this. Somehow God must be able to turn evil on its head and bring good out of it. Somehow God must be able to take even the most horrific of tragedies and bring them to a happy ending. In John Paul's book, what begins as a philosophical study of evil incarnate in history merges into a broader theological reflection on the roots of evil itself and the victory of redemption. In the mind of this pope, evil has never been total or absolute. It is always, he says, circumscribed by good. "If redemption marks the divine limit placed upon evil," he writes, "it is for this reason only: because thereby evil is radically overcome by good, hate by love, death by resurrection." Saint Augustine had a great way of expressing this too: "For God judged it better to bring good out of evil than not to permit any evil to exist."[1]

I often think that this is the great revelation of Good Friday. This yearly commemoration marks the greatest evil in human history: the day we put God to death. It signifies humanity's rejection of love, purity, innocence, and goodness when we strung up God and nailed him to a wooden cross. And yet, from the pinnacle of human evil God wrought the greatest good: our redemption. As Joseph Ratzinger once wrote, "In the abyss of human failure is revealed the still more inexhaustible abyss of divine love."[2] God took evil and exploded it from within, turning its venom to nectar and its sting into a healing balm.

If God is able to bring forth this immense good from the evil of Good Friday, he can surely turn all the lesser evils of our lives into surprise packages of unexpected grace.

∞

Jesus, I don't know why certain things have happened to me or why people whom I love have to suffer so much, but today I reaffirm my faith that you do know why. Lord, I promise to move forward with the assurance that you will bring forth a greater good out of every instance of evil and suffering in my life and in this world. I love you, Jesus.

CHAPTER 7

We Have Everything We Need

❦

WHEN DO YOU start packing your luggage before a long trip? My friends give me a hard time because I'm usually packing on the way to the airport. As you might guess, I also give myself *plenty* of time to arrive *just* before the airline closes the gate. We all have different styles. I'm duly impressed by people who start packing their bag, little by little, a week or two before their departure date just to make sure they don't forget any of the essentials.

Although I would like to think my style is more balanced, exhibiting less of a need to control every detail, I know it's not. In fact, I'm pretty sure that my risk-taking and spontaneous style is just another expression of the same desire to control every outcome that I criticize in the early packers. I am determined not to pack my bags ahead of time because there are many other things demanding my attention that I must control first.

If we are healthy human beings, we like to be in control. It is a survival instinct. Yet the serenity that we ask God for is a serenity found through relinquishing our futile attempts at controlling the uncontrollable. We are asking God for the serenity to let go of the reins when hanging on to them is doing us no good anyway.

An important step toward achieving this serenity comes through realizing that we need very little to be successful and happy. Some time ago I was struck by a passage in the Gospel that had never meant much to me before. After first giving them their marching orders, Jesus sends out the seventy-two disciples, in pairs, on their first mission to prepare for his visits to different towns around Palestine. The surprising thing is that he doesn't equip them—he strips them. He takes away not only many superfluous things, but even things we would consider useful and even necessary. His instructions are as specific as they are bizarre: "Take nothing for your journey, no staff, nor bag, nor bread, nor money—not even an extra tunic" (Luke 9:3).

When we travel, we make a mental list of all the things we will need: our toothbrush, pajamas, passport, iPad, breviary, jacket—the list goes on and on. But Jesus seems more worried about the disciples taking too much rather than forgetting something important. What is the deal here? Why does Jesus insist on this radical austerity? He is teaching them, and us, to trust. He wants the disciples to be uncluttered and even a little insecure, so that they will rely more on God's providence than on the contents of their backpacks. We never really learn how much God cares for us until we let go of the many securities that sustain us in our lives.

God never promises to give us everything we desire in life. But much of what we desire isn't much good for us anyway. Even the Rolling Stones reached this simple conclusion: "You can't always get what you want, but if you try sometimes you just might find . . . you get what you need." God does not over-equip us for our mission in life, but nothing is lacking either. Sure, we'd love the latest technology, the best-trained staff, an unlimited budget, and yet we find ourselves with only a few rudimentary tools for tackling what seems to be a gargantuan task. This is the way God seems to like it.

The same holds true for our personal lives. When we take inventory of our gifts and talents, we often come up short. We find that we lack many of the qualities that other people have, qualities that would be very helpful for our mission in life. We have moral disabilities, flawed characters, and imperfect personalities. And yet, this is how God made us and he still expects big things of us!

When we ask for serenity to accept the things we cannot change, we ask to be able to do without the things that God doesn't want us to have and to embrace our dependence on him.

Saint Augustine observed that "no matter how rich a man is on earth, he is still God's beggar."[1] Every time we pray the Lord's Prayer, we are reminded of our status as God's beggars. We come to him cap in hand. Moreover, we don't ask for an abundance. We request "our daily bread," not bread for the coming month. This means, of course, that we will be back tomorrow to make the same request. We live not of ourselves, but of the goodness of his daily dispensations.

It seems clear to me that God wills us to always feel a little insecure in ourselves and in worldly promises so that we will find our true security in him. He shakes things up from time to time to remind us how much we need him. And he does this, I am convinced, not to belittle us but to raise us up. Rather than place our trust in things or people that will fail us in the end, he wants us to place our trust where it belongs. Indeed, at the core of our serenity is the conviction that we already have everything we need.

∞

Lord, today I go forward in confidence knowing that with you at my side I have everything I need to do what I should. Out of love for you, I now let go of every ounce of fear. For you, Lord, are enough for me.

CHAPTER 8

The Allure of Material Possessions

◈

OR MANY YEARS, a friend of mine was a lot like King Midas: everything Bob touched in real estate turned to gold. Leading up to the financial crisis of 2008, he and his wife Christine were doing so well that even though they both came from a humble background, they started traveling by private jet, since they now were accustomed to nothing but the best. All of that changed in 2008. Despite Bob's best efforts to plan ahead (keeping large cash reserves, limiting his exposure), he simply couldn't anticipate the deep impact of the crisis. Suddenly, not only was his company at risk, but so were many of the family assets.

The unexpected part of Bob and Christine's story is how it affected them spiritually. They had always been people of faith and practicing Christians. They thought they had deep reserves of trust in God. Yet when the Great Recession hit their pocketbooks, suddenly that faith and trust were shaken to the core. Doubt started growing in their hearts, and bitterness replaced the easygoing spirit in them that I had known. I tried my best to stay close to them during their trial, but at a certain point they shut off most contact with me, saying that God had not protected them from the crisis.

I can think of equally prosperous families who went through similar crises and came out more in love with God than ever before. What makes the difference can be found in our attitude toward the material blessings God gives us.

A certain detachment from material possessions is necessary to achieve the serenity we seek. Riches can become an "idol" that tests our allegiance to God and our trust in him. Wealth can make us feel stronger, surer, more powerful—and sometimes even superior to others. Those who have a lot can rest easy, with no worry for where their next meal is coming from. The poor cannot.

A simple question we can ask ourselves to determine whether we are attached to a material good is whether or not this item is helping us get closer to heaven. If it is not, and still we won't let it go, we are attached.

When Jesus recommends that his followers be "poor in spirit," his desire is not to see us sad, but to see us happy. Spiritual poverty is detachment from anything that might get in the way of our attachment to God and his will for us. Christ chose radical poverty for himself as a path to union with his Father. He was born in a stable, with no more royal court than some poor shepherds and animals. He lived free of attachments to material things, so much so that his very food was to do the will of his Father (see John 4:34). He had no place to call his own, nowhere even to lay his head (see Luke 9:58). He died poor too, on a rough wooden cross, surrounded by thieves, and his body was eventually laid in a borrowed tomb (see Matthew 27:60).

When we imitate Christ in his poverty, we also share in his peace. A Christian who lives with his treasure in heaven and his trust in God is spared many of the anxieties that this world brings.

In the Psalms we read of men who trust in riches. In the end they find their trust betrayed and their hopes dashed. "The righteous will see, and fear, and will laugh at the evildoer, saying, 'See the one who would not take refuge in God, but trusted in abundant riches, and sought refuge in wealth!'" (Psalm 52:6–7).

Spiritual poverty—detachment from anything that doesn't point us toward heaven—has another important function. It allows us an interior liberty that frees us from needless worries and concerns. The Spanish mystic John of the Cross offered an interesting analogy to show how attachments can keep us from being truly free. He says that any attachment at all, even a small one, can hold us back from the freedom that God intends for us. He compares us to a bird that longs to fly but is tied by the leg and cannot leave the ground. "For it comes to the same thing whether a bird be held by a slender cord or by a stout one; since, even if it be slender, the bird will be well held as though it were stout, for so long as it breaks it not and flies not away."[1]

The sort of poverty that Jesus asks of us is not a punishment, but a gift. It does not bind us—it frees us. It allows us to walk through this world as pilgrims who know that our homeland is somewhere else. Spiritual poverty keeps us from becoming overjoyed over our worldly gains or unduly distraught over our worldly losses.

Jesus promised that the truth would set us free (see John 8:32). A true Christian is liberated from the unbearable weight of earthly anxiety. Our faith enables us to take the "slings and arrows of outrageous fortune" in stride, neither rejoicing too much over what has little eternal value nor weeping too much when worldly treasures fail. Look how beautifully Saint Paul expressed the freedom and peace of soul that this inner detachment brings:

> *I have learned to be content with whatever I have. I know what it is to have little, and I know what it is to have plenty. In any and all circumstances I have learned the secret of being well-fed and of going hungry, of having plenty and of being in need. I can do all things through him who strengthens me. (Philippians 4:11–13)*

Yet this inner freedom doesn't just happen; it is the fruit of real choices. We need to consciously opt for Christ and opt against dependence on the world. Affective poverty (poverty of the heart) needs to have an effective expression (poverty in practice). To experience the joy of the Lord, we need to cut excess things and activities out of our lives, including anything that binds or overly distracts us. Even good things are bad for us when they become too important to us, when we feel as if we couldn't or wouldn't want to live without them.

When we simplify, we de-clutter our relationship with God and free our minds and hearts for love. Such freedom translates immediately into serenity of soul.

∞

Thank you, O God, for all material blessings you have given to me. They are undeserved and unnecessary. Free my heart from any attachment to things that will be here today and gone tomorrow, that I might be free to love you and love others without measure.

CHAPTER 9

Climb a Mountain, Then Look Again

❦

ONE OF CINEMA'S most memorable portrayals of all time is Julie Andrews's stunning performance as Maria von Trapp in the classic 1965 musical *The Sound of Music*. And if any scene from the film deserves the title of "iconic," it is Maria whirling about in the Austrian Alps singing, "The hills are alive with the sound of music." High above the doldrums of daily existence in the valleys below, Maria found freedom in the open, cool air of the mountains. In those hills she found liberty and transcendence and gained a new perspective on her day-to-day life.

When we look down from the heights—literally or figuratively—we can see things that escape us in our day-to-day hustle to keep our heads above water. It gives us perspective, and perspective helps us find serenity even at times when circumstances may be unchangeable and less than ideal.

As long as we are caught up in the day-to-day, life can seem like an unending stream of hearing the baby cry, fixing the broken radiator, going to work, coming home from work, driving the kids to soccer, not getting enough sleep, wondering why our spouse seems not to love us as before, and so on. The apparent meaninglessness of our daily occupations is one of the most suffocating of prisons. Like a factory worker whose sole task is to put the same nut on the same bolt thousands of times a day, we can feel that every day is the same, even as our days are running out.

It is an exaggeration to say that everything is a matter of perspective, but it is true that most events and circumstances in our lives can be viewed in different ways. And often a change in perspective radically alters our evaluation of things. One of the most important tools we have for gaining a new and more objective perspective is distance. The old adage about not being able to see the forest for the trees is very apt for most of us. We are so immersed in our own troubles that we can see nothing else. Our difficulties are so evident that they conceal our blessings. When we back away from those troubles, however, we begin to gain a more balanced view of them.

I experienced this in a profound way when I requested from the superiors of my former religious order a six-month leave of absence in order to work in a parish in New York City and discern whether God was calling me to make a major vocational change in my life, from a religious order (missionary work) to the diocesan priesthood (local parish). Upon arriving in New York, I knew almost immediately that I should transition out of the religious order. I didn't expect such clarity. It was as if scales fell from my eyes and I could see things I never saw before. During the many years I had been part of this religious order—the Legionaries of Christ—I had been unable to see, or had not wanted to see, the obvious dysfunction and mind manipulation that was present at many levels of the organization. False assumptions I had held for many years quickly fell apart. Healthier ways of approaching the same spiritual goals

I'd always had became instantly evident. I was able to reconsider some of the rash judgments I had made of people and other institutions and begin to see them more as Jesus sees them and, when appropriate, to ask for their forgiveness. Not all of this new light streamed into my mind and heart overnight, but a great deal of it did. That was a miracle. That was God doing what I could never do. All I needed was a new perch, a new mountain from which to look down and see the obvious. But to get there I needed to climb the mountain.

I should add that from this new place of reflection I was able to see not only what was wrong with my prior circumstances, but also the tremendous good that was there, especially the wonderful people who surrounded me.

You will notice that Jesus often went off to the mountaintop or the desert to pray. He put physical distance between himself and the day-to-day occupations of his public ministry in order to talk with his Father and regain a clear vision of what he was about. In a desert, the starkness of the surroundings and the absence of many comforts force us to engage with what is most essential. On the mountain, the cares of our daily lives look very small and insignificant, and we gain a perspective on their place in a much broader scheme of things. We also gain the serenity to accept the things we cannot change.

As Christians we are called to have a "sacramental" view of reality, meaning that behind our day-to-day lives is a deeper reality. The circumstances of our lives point us beyond themselves to spiritual truths and reveal the handiwork of God. This is true not only of extraordinary events—like baptism— but also of the most humdrum daily activities of our lives. God is at work not only on the altar and in the operating room but also, as Saint Teresa of Ávila would say, "amongst the pots and pans"![1] He is to be found everywhere, active and eager for us to find him. If he is active among the pots and pans, then he is surely also active in the classroom, in the nursery, in the office, in the car, in the boardroom, in the kitchen, and on the sports field. He wants us to open our eyes of faith to discover him and to live in his presence.

It's hard for modern men and women to escape to the mountains to regain perspective, but we can find little substitute mountains that allow us the distance we need. The most important of these is daily prayer. Fifteen minutes in God's presence can be the difference between seeing nothing but grief and grayness in our day and seeing the light of God's abundant mercies. Being with God is being in heaven. From there, the meaning of everything else grows clearer. In a way, life's hills are alive with "the sound of music"—the music of God's loving activity. In this divine context and vision, in this embrace of God's vision, isn't it easier to imagine accepting serenely those difficult things we cannot change?

∞

Heavenly Father, you know I am caught up in many things. You know all that I have on my mind and how distracted I am from the spiritual world. Today, accompany me all the way that I might see as you see, judge as you judge, love as you love.

CHAPTER 10

Serenity Is Possible No Matter What Comes Our Way

୧୫

I T IS RELATIVELY EASY to be serene in those rare moments when everything is going our way, and quite another thing to be serene when we are beset by all sorts of difficulties that we cannot make go away or change to our liking.

The spiritual strength to maintain serenity in bad times, and especially in the worst of times, comes from one place, and one place only: the faith conviction that if we are being tried, it is by God's loving permission, and that, if we let him, he will bring forth from our trial a greater good than anything we could ever imagine.

Although I've written a whole book on the topic of suffering—specifically, on how to tap into God's purpose and plan for when life hurts—nowhere have I seen greater proof of serenity in impossibly difficult circumstances than in my friend Thomas Peters. Thom is a young, bright light in the field of political and religious punditry and activism. Last year he married a wonderful young woman and then, three months later, suffered a life-threatening diving accident. After several months of intensive care, surgeries, and therapy, this is what he wrote:[1]

"On a Friday in July I awoke in the early morning hours to someone beating on my back with their fists. I was lying on a bed in a place I did not recognize and I was in excruciating pain. It was a kind of pain I had never experienced before and did not understand. There was a tube down my throat and my body felt incomplete, as if much of it was missing. I came to realize in the hours that followed, the man beating on my back with his fists was a nurse, and he was trying to dislodge some of the fluid that was filling up my lungs as the result of the diving accident I had sustained three days previously, an accident that had fractured my fifth vertebra and had given me a severe spinal cord injury, an injury that has changed the course of my life forever. I have no memory of the accident itself. By God's grace, someone spotted me floating facedown in the water and started dragging me to the shore. Had I not been seen, I would have surely died. By God's grace, I was injured on one of the only two days of the year when a group of EMTs gathered less than a mile away for training, so I received prompt medical care for my drowning damage. Had it not been that particular day, help would have been about twenty minutes away and I would have sustained brain damage. And by God's grace, there was a field nearby large enough for a rescue helicopter to land and transport me to the University of Maryland Medical Center's Shock Trauma Center, the best unit of its kind in North America. Had I not received the benefit of the best possible care so soon, my recovery would have been unalterably impaired. Recovery was, and is, hard. It took six weeks to patch me up to a medically stable position suitable enough to transfer me to a rehabilitation center in Washington, DC. For six weeks in Baltimore, nurses and doctors battled infections and secretions to heal the damage my lungs had suffered from ingesting filthy water. I was placed in a metal halo in an effort to save my fractured vertebra. And when that effort ultimately failed, I underwent a two-day surgery to replace the damaged vertebra with a titanium cage. The surgeons also fused my fourth and sixth vertebrae to strengthen my neck. I was intubated, given a tracheotomy, re-intubated, and put back on the tracheotomy.

"A steady stream of friends and family visited me during this time to lift my spirits and to share tears and smiles. But no one was more faithful than my wife Natalie; she did not leave my side my entire time in the Intensive Care Unit.

"A major accident is an invitation to both physical and spiritual recovery. I have never felt God's presence as much as I do since the accident. People will say that accidents like mine should call into question God's mercy or even His existence. But for me, the fact that I survived my injury is the greatest evidence I have ever experienced of God's mercy and providence. I believe God allowed my accident to happen and that He chose to help me survive that accident and every day gives me the opportunity to be blessed through it. The accident has taught me the essential value defended by the principle of subsidiarity: the value of family and friends as the first line of defense when things go badly. My family and friends have come forward to help my wife and I in ways that have taken our breath away. They brought us meals, helped pack and move our home, loaned us their cars, contributed their professional advice like how to plan our financial future and cover medical expenses, they have organized prayer groups for us, designed wristbands to help remind people to pray for us and offered us gifts so generous I have had to firmly say no because they are simply too much.

"The man is never poor or alone who has good friends. My wife and I simply could not have survived this were it not for our dear family and friends. The accident has taught me more about the incredible gift of marriage. My father, during his speech at my wedding reception, said the sacrament of marriage gives us the grace to do the impossible. I have met people during these months who think it is incredible, even impossible, that my wife and I survived a trauma like this having been married only three months. I tell them it helps to marry the right woman and get married the right way, the way the Church taught the two of us what marriage is and why it should be honored. People have told us that they are inspired and receive hope from the witness of our marriage—it inspires us too, I respond! We feel it is possible to face anything, even a future of me paralyzed, so long as we cling to each other, to God, and to our marriage vows.

"The accident has taught me to be more humble and realistic about my own efforts and contributions. Before my accident I took pride in my self-reliance, and my ability to contribute to the causes I care about, and I still do, but since the accident I have gained a far greater appreciation for the fact that everything I do and am is because of the Lord. I certainly didn't bring myself back from the brink of death and, as a wise priest told me, my prayers and sacrifices these weeks and months have done more to aid the causes of life, marriage and religious freedom than anything I wrote, said or did to promote these prior to the accident. But make no mistake, as soon as I am able, I am coming back to fight harder than ever for all of these things because I know now that it is prayer that makes the warrior his strongest.

"The accident has taught me that I am a work still in progress and anything I do achieve is for God's glory. I completed my term of inpatient rehabilitation this week and the hard work of learning to live on my own again (with the tremendous help of my wife) has just begun, as has grueling outpatient therapy to regain more of the strength and muscle systems I have lost.

"The vast, vast majority of individuals with my injury never walk again, but there remain signs that I could beat these long odds, and I have been praying to Saint Jude for such a miracle. The majority of individuals with an injury like mine never regain the use of their hands—I have had to write these reflections using a knuckle of my right pinky on a touchscreen, if you can believe it. But through the intercession of Saint Francis, I am recovering some finger function in my left hand. There are troubling signs that my life will forever be plagued with neuropathic pain, but as I have learned, pain can be offered up and need not inhibit living a good and worthy life.

"In the coming months, I will be focusing on prayer, reflection and recovery, and then we will know more about what the future holds. I don't quite remember how it began, but during one of the many sleepless nights spent in the Baltimore ICU, unsure of what that night and the next day would hold, I was inspired by the example of Samuel in the Old Testament, and began quietly saying to God, 'Speak, Lord, your servant is listening.' This remains my prayer. I do not know what the future holds. But I do know that as long as I have breath, and with whatever limbs and muscles I can move, I will strive to serve the Lord and do His will. What else is a life for?"

God never wills evil; he didn't cause Thom's accident. But he does allow us to pass through a very imperfect world where the laws of fallen nature and the abuse of free will wreak havoc on the righteous and evil alike. What we do with our trials depends on us. Whether we choose to live in bitterness and resentment or trust in God's providential care depends on us.

And in play in that choice to reject or accept the things we cannot change is our serenity of soul.

Saint Augustine wrote: "Our pilgrimage on earth cannot be exempt from trial. We progress by means of trial. No one knows himself except through trial, or receives a crown except after victory, or strives except against an enemy or temptations."[2] In other words, in light of eternity, however painful our trials may be, they can bring great rewards to our lives as we learn to live serenely in the knowledge of God's power and care.

The Bible takes great pains to assure us that Jesus was tried in every way that we are. Every Lent we read of his temptations in the desert and how he came through them victorious. He is our strength and the guarantor of our own victory. Moreover, Saint Paul assures us that we will not be tempted beyond our strength. God is not unjust and never allows anything that we cannot handle, with his grace.

That great saint and scholar Thomas Aquinas, in one of the many prayers he left us, asks God that neither triumphs nor difficult ordeals should disturb his peace or alter his resolve. "Grant, Lord my God," he writes, "that I may never fall away in success or in failure; that I may not be prideful in prosperity nor dejected in adversity. Let me rejoice only in what unites us and sorrow only in what separates us."[3]

∞

Jesus, the trials on my plate seem to get bigger with time. These I accept today as part of your plan for me. I don't reject them. I accept them as an essential part of my journey toward you. Give me your grace to live these beloved trials gracefully.

CHAPTER 11

Owning Our History

༄

I SPOKE EARLIER about Alcoholics Anonymous, the twelve-step program that has transformed so many lives. The first three steps ask us to acknowledge our own powerlessness and to recognize God's power to heal. The next three steps move in a slightly different direction. They demand a radical honesty, a sort of "confession" of where we are and how we got there.

The fourth step entails making "a searching and fearless moral inventory of ourselves." What a great line! This "fearless moral inventory" consists in what many spiritual teachers have called an "examination of conscience" in which we lay bare our lives and honestly face up to who we are and what we have done. This radical honesty is essential for moving forward.

The fifth step goes further and makes us less comfortable still, though it is deeply healing. We are invited to admit "to God, to ourselves, and to another human being the exact nature of our wrongs." Yikes, that is tough. It is one thing to generally acknowledge that we aren't perfect or that there are many things we should change in our lives. It is another thing altogether to spell that out in detail to another human being. However difficult the fifth step is, it is also remarkably effective. In the Catholic Church, we do something very similar in the Sacrament of Reconciliation: through a priest, we ask God for forgiveness and strength to avoid sin in the future. But for both Catholics and non-Catholic Christians, it is also helpful, even important, to have a spiritual director or accountability partner with whom we can discuss our struggles, temptations, and spiritual progress.

Finally, turning again to God, the sixth step has us asking him for readiness to have him "remove all these defects of character." We see once again that God alone is the one who can fix all that is broken and heal all that is wounded. This sixth step may seem unnecessary, since who wouldn't want his defects wiped away? But in reality, we often don't want to lose all our defects. We are attached to them. Saint Augustine famously prayed to God: "Lord, give me chastity, but not yet."[1] It takes courage to sincerely ask God to change us now.

The serenity to accept the things we cannot change entails acknowledging the choices we have made and the consequences of those choices. We cannot move forward until we do. As hard as it is, we must "come clean" and face the reality of our life without pulling any punches. Just as a doctor can't heal us until we explain what is wrong, so too peace of soul comes at the price of brutal honesty with ourselves and with God.

Jesus famously declared that the truth would set us free (John 8:32). But what does this mean? In what sense does the truth liberate human beings? In what way is the "truth" a door to human freedom? Human beings, it would seem, are the only creatures capable of lying. It is true that other animals "disguise" themselves by blending into their surroundings or by seeming to be something they are not. Chameleons change color to match their surroundings, and the appearances of some insects, like the walking stick, mimic their surroundings so perfectly that they are rendered virtually invisible. Dogs, it would seem, get pretty close to lying when they hide after being naughty. Yet in the animal kingdom we are dealing more with evolutionary survival tactics than with conscious acts of deceit. We humans, on the other hand, can willingly and knowingly misrepresent ourselves and seek to make others believe something we ourselves know not to be true.

More seriously still, we humans have the ability not only to tell a lie but also to "live" a lie, making deceit the very bed we lie in and the home we dwell in. We can even deceive ourselves, rationalizing our errors and convincing ourselves that we are better than we really are. But these lies we tell and live in are in fact a prison. To live in falsehood is to live imprisoned in unreality. Have you noticed that when people unburden themselves of lies they have been carrying they inevitably feel a sense of deep relief and liberation? They suddenly feel like they can breathe after suffocating for who knows how long in the grip of falsehood. Lies weigh on us like great boulders on our heads and shoulders, and we ache to cast them away.

Of all the lies we tell others or ourselves, the most dangerous concern our own choices and decisions. Our knee-jerk reaction is to justify ourselves, defend ourselves, rationalize our choices. Yet in the end this is our downfall.

Conversion away from a life based in lies does not require that we tell everyone about every one of our past sins before we can start living truthfully again. I once heard Oprah Winfrey tell her audience (yes, that's a confession!) that sometimes deciding to "tell all" is in fact the selfish choice. We might feel very good when we unburden ourselves of secrets by dumping them on our spouse, on our blog, or on our best friend, but if we are doing it mostly for ourselves, we aren't doing the right thing. Selfless love is always our standard.

Last year I had the grace of getting to know Judy Clark, an inmate at the Bedford Hills Correctional Facility for Women in New York. Hers is a fascinating story of conversion that passes through the gate of humble acceptance of personal failings. The story doesn't begin well. On October 20, 1981, a group of radicals armed with automatic weapons attempted to rob an armored Brink's truck at Nanuet Mall in Nanuet, New York. The robbers took $1.6 million in cash and gunned down one of the Brink's guards, Peter Paige, as well as two police officers, Waverly Brown and Edward O'Grady. Judith Alice Clark was the getaway driver.

Judy was arrested that same day and indicted on three counts of second-degree murder. When she finally appeared in court for the closing arguments, she merely confirmed her guilt. "Revolutionary violence is necessary, and it is a liberating force," she told the jury. Judy was found guilty and sentenced to three consecutive terms of twenty-five years to life. At the time of her arrest, Judy was thirty-one years old, the mother of an eleven-month-old baby, and a member of the "May 19" Communist organization—a small, tightly knit, self-defined "revolutionary anti-imperialist organization." By her own admission, her political activity, loyalty to her "comrades," and identity as a "revolutionary" had been the defining reality of her entire adult life.

Now things are very different for Judy. During her long years of confinement, Judy came to understand that brutal honesty with herself was central to her process of renewal. She began opening her heart and mind to the reality of what she had done and to the possibility of becoming a different person. She writes: "My life in prison has been, to a great extent, defined by my coming to grips with the pain and losses I am responsible for, and my efforts to atone and build a life rooted in remorse, repair, and reverence for all life." By acknowledging what she had done and its effects on other people's lives, Judy found the door to redemption. This has borne great fruit in her life.

At the date of this writing, Judy has served thirty-two years of her prison sentence. While in prison, she earned a bachelor's degree in behavioral sciences in 1990 and a master's degree in psychology in 1993, and is now working on her PhD. She has taught prenatal parenting classes for pregnant women and been a mentor and role model to the nursery mothers who live with their babies in a special unit in the prison. Judy helped rebuild a prison college program when public funding for it was eliminated in the 1990s. As a result, more than 150 women have been awarded associate's or bachelor's degrees in the past ten years. Judy lives in a special volunteer unit with inmates who participate in the Puppies Behind Bars Program. She raises and trains puppies to become guide dogs for the blind, explosive detection dogs for law enforcement agencies, and service dogs for disabled veterans. And in response to an AIDS epidemic in the town of Bedford Hills (the site of the prison) during the 1980s, Judy cofounded ACE, an organization so effective that it has been replicated in prisons across the country.

All of this came about because she finally owned up to the truth of her life. Far from bringing her down, this acknowledgment lifted her up. At her trial, Judy had defended her actions tooth and nail. The wrongs of society were everyone else's fault, not hers. Yet after some time in prison thinking about her actions, Judy was forced to confront the truth that she had done wrong. Listen to the words she speaks now:

"I am deeply ashamed of my actions, which contributed to the deaths of three innocent men and physical and emotional injuries and losses to many others. I have spent a good part of my years in prison trying to understand the inner and external forces that propelled me into such self-destructive, anti-human behavior. I am now trying to live on very different, more responsible terms."

In upcoming chapters, I will share more of what I have learned from inmate Judy Clark. It isn't easy owning up to our own failings. These are the hardest truths to recognize. Still, we all have them. We all are capable of great evil, and we deceive ourselves to think we are not. Not all of us rob banks or commit murder, but we all have things to be sorry for. The fact that we aren't notorious criminals does not mean we are innocent. Part of the serenity we seek involves accepting our own past, our own choices (good and bad), and the consequences of those choices. These are truly the things we cannot change, and we need serenity to accept them for what they are.

∞

Lord, I thank you for the gift of my life, for all the years you have given me on this beautiful earth. I am deeply sorry for the many times I have abused this gift by living selfishly. Please wipe away my shame and give me grace to move on with renewed zeal to live in truth and love.

CHAPTER 12

God Loves You, Warts and All

❧

DESPITE WHAT I said earlier about mosquitoes, God doesn't make mistakes. Most importantly for our purposes here, God made no mistakes when creating you. You are exactly what he intended for you to be. Everything about you—your parents, your siblings, your moment in history, your neighborhood, your qualities and defects—all of these were allowed by God's providence. You are known and loved by God, warts and all. Is that not the greatest motivation ever to be serene?

An encouraging corollary to this truth is that even your defects are used by God. What you find most embarrassing, God now finds essential for your mission in life. What you find to be your greatest weakness, God sees as an opportunity for strength. What you see as an obstacle, God sees as a stepping-stone. Saint Paul realized this in his own life, and the discovery gave him great joy. He experienced what he metaphorically described as a "thorn in his flesh," and he begged God to remove it. And yet God answered him: "My grace is sufficient for you, for power is made perfect in weakness" (2 Corinthians

12:9). And from this Paul concludes: "Therefore I am content with weaknesses, insults, hardships, persecutions, and calamities for the sake of Christ; for whenever I am weak, then I am strong" (2 Corinthians 12:10).

When you look at yourself in the mirror and see a poor, deeply flawed creature who is quite incapable of good works, in that moment God sees you as an instrument of his grace. You have reached a deeper enlightenment than the person who sees in himself a talented, capable individual whom God should be privileged to have on his team. During the concluding mass of the Toronto World Youth Day in 2002, Pope John Paul II spoke words that remind us of God's power to renew us. "We are not the sum of our weaknesses and failures," he declared, "we are the sum of the Father's love for us and our real capacity to become the image of his son."[1]

There is a lovely story in the Old Testament that bears this out beautifully. Everyone knows the story of David and Goliath, how the young, inexperienced shepherd boy defeats the seasoned soldier—a giant no less! What you may not recall is what happens in the moment before David takes to the field of battle (see I Samuel 17:38–39). He has no protection from the enemy, no armor to wear, so King Saul lends him his armor. Saul puts a bronze helmet on David's head and clothes him in a coat of mail. But this doesn't work for David. He realizes that he can't even walk wearing Saul's heavy armor, and he has to take it off. He ends up going out to meet Goliath with nothing but a sling and a few smooth stones. And yet, with God's help, he wins.

One of the lessons here is that what we sometimes see as our strength turns out to be our weakness. It gets in our way. When we feel more helpless, we rely more fully on God's grace, and he works miracles in us. Heavy armor is not David's strength. His small stature and his agility turn out to be assets, yet no one knows this until he takes the field. What seem to be our greatest defects often turn out to be the tool God was counting on to get the job done.

Do you see why, in the light of faith, we have every reason to serenely accept the things we cannot change? If God has his way—that is, if we let him do his work—they will become the bridge we take to cross over turbulent waters.

When I consider God's ways, I think he must have a sense of humor. Who would ever choose Moses, a stutterer, to be his mouthpiece before all of Israel and before Pharaoh? When Moses received this call, he must have thought, *You have got to be kidding, right? You really couldn't have found anyone a little better qualified?* Yet God wasn't kidding. He knew what He was doing. So many saints felt woefully unprepared and even unqualified for what they were asked to do. Sticking to biblical examples, we can think of God's choice of Gideon, a common farmer, to deliver Israel from Midian. Or Rahab, a prostitute, who enabled Joshua to conquer Jericho. The disciples themselves—a group of uncouth fishermen—were completely unqualified for founding the Church. Not one had the training for such an enterprise, and they all had deep moral flaws as well.

All of this is summed up nicely in Saint Paul's beautiful statement: "God has chosen the foolish things of the world to put to shame the wise, and God has chosen the weak things of the world to put to shame the things which are mighty; and the base things of the world and the things which are despised God has chosen, and the things which are not, to bring to nothing the things that are, that no flesh should glory in His presence" (1 Corinthians 1:27–29). God's favorite instruments are nobodies, so that no man can boast before God. We can be serene accepting the things we cannot change, knowing that God can use even our weaknesses to show his power and our blemishes to manifest his beauty.

∞

Oh God, you know how much my weakness bothers me.
You know how inadequate I feel for what you ask of me.
Today I am going to embrace fully who I am and who
I am not. I would only ask that you show me how much
you love me, warts and all.

CHAPTER 13

God's Mercy Has No Limits

❧

ONE OF THE biggest obstacles to putting our trust in God is that we have so irreparably messed things up. We have so shattered the china vase of our lives (and sometimes the lives of others) that even the best potter couldn't possibly repair it. Even if someone were able to collect all those shards and figure out how they originally fit together, it would be futile to try to do so. We are like Humpty Dumpty—all the king's horses and all the king's men cannot possibly put us together again. Popular wisdom says that "what's done is done," and from a purely human perspective, that is true. What is done cannot be undone. We see the scars on our soul, the harm that we have caused, and we despair of this damage ever being set right again. How can we possibly be serene in the face of such unchangeable tragedy?

Yet here we have the greatest miracle of God's mercy. It seems altogether too good to be true, and we are afraid to believe it. God is able to right our wrongs and recast the china vase of our lives. He does so over and over again. He takes even our seemingly unpardonable sins and turns them to good. This is the mystery of redemption.

The beautiful little saint of Lisieux, Saint Therese, was known for her boundless trust in the goodness of God. She found it quite natural to expect everything from him, convinced as she was of his great love for her. That's hard for us because, unlike this innocent young girl, we have offended God too many times and in too many ways. Yet Therese would disagree that our sin should be an obstacle to trust in God. She made clear that her confidence in the infinite goodness and mercy of God had nothing whatsoever to do with her own moral track record. She took pains to insist:

Yes, I sense that even if I had on my conscience all the sins which can be committed, I would go, my heart broken, to repent and throw myself into the arms of Jesus, for I know how much He cherishes the prodigal child who returns to Him.

Again, shortly before her death, speaking to Mother Agnes, she said,

You may truly say that if I had committed all possible crimes, I would still have the same confidence; I would feel that this multitude of offenses would be like a drop of water thrown into a flaming furnace.[1]

The reason for this is really very simple. The source of our trust in God is not our good works, as if God were merciful and generous because *we* are so good and deserving, but simply because *he* is that good. His mercy shines most clearly right when we deserve it least. We never earn his mercy; it comes as a free and undeserved gift. This is an important message for all of us, both those who are "big" sinners and those who are only aware of smaller faults. God does not love us more or less depending on how well we perform. He loves us totally and completely and unconditionally, which means that God's love doesn't depend on anything else. It is unchanging, and nothing we do or don't do can alter that.

It has always consoled me to think that Jesus came to call sinners. He specifically says that sinners are the reason he came to earth and the reason he died on the cross. He defends his friendship with sinners by saying that healthy people don't need a physician; only sick people do. I am happy to recognize myself as one of those needy ones, because it allows me to enter into the intimate circle of Jesus's friends.

One early Saturday morning not long ago I was waiting for a train at Penn Station to head to a beach on the south shore of Long Island. It was my day off, and I was in casual clothes. As I sat at a cafeteria-style table eating a breakfast sandwich, a gentleman came up to me, presumably to ask for money. He didn't even give me time to debate what I should do: "Sir, I would love to have some breakfast too. Can you give me five bucks?"

"Well, sir," I responded, "how about I buy you one of these sandwiches?"

"That is very kind of you, sir, but I buy my breakfast around the corner. I always get a low-fat bran muffin with whipped cream on top."

I chuckled to myself, quite impressed with both his audacity and his breakfast menu. I noticed another patron watching all of this go down. As I reached into my pocket this patron let out an audible groan, as if to say, *You're crazy!* More out of laziness than kindness, I decided to take a risk: "Sir, I'm going to give you some money to go buy your breakfast. I would only ask that you bring back the receipt." The only bill I had in my pocket was a twenty. I'm not sure who was more shocked, my fellow patron or the man with extravagant culinary taste asking for money.

Five minutes passed and I was about to leave. I knew I would have to look at the street-smart New Yorker at the other table and admit defeat. But then in walked our friend with a low-fat bran muffin with whipped cream on top in one hand and some bills, coins, and a receipt in the other. With a smirk on his face, he looked at me and said, "Your change, sir. Have a good day." I don't remember if I resisted looking over at the other patron. Probably not. As I accepted the change I told this man how much he had inspired me. Not everyone, I said, would have done what he just did, and he was a very good man. I then told him that I was a priest. "What's that?" he said.

"I'm a minister. You know, a pastor."

His eyes got big, and he let out a scream as he left the restaurant: "I have won the Jesus lottery!" I was in joyful shock. And the man at the other table couldn't resist some commentary: "I have never witnessed anything more beautiful than that."

I believe the low-fat bran muffin man really did win the Jesus lottery. He did the right thing and saw his moral triumph as a sign of God's mercy in his life.

It is sometimes said that life is like photography: we use the negatives to develop the picture. This seems to hold true for our sins, as long as we learn from them. Jesus tells Mary Magdalene that he does not condemn her. Of course, he doesn't condone her sin either. He simply says: "Go and sin no more."

We have said that an important part of Christian faith is an awareness of God's power to turn evil into good. This is especially evident in the case of our sins. Look at what Francis de Sales says about sin: "The scorpion that stings us is poisonous when it does so. But made into an oil it becomes a powerful remedy against its own sting. Sin is shameful only at the time we commit it. Changed into confession and repentance, it is honorable and brings salvation."[2] It is not the nature of sin, which is evil and ugly, that makes this true, but the power of God, who is infinite mercy.

In the life of grace, no error is final. God will always welcome us back, no matter what our past may look like and no matter how many pockmarks there are on our soul. Where there's life there's hope. And, we may add, where there is hope there is serenity.

∞

Lord, I know I have won the Jesus lottery. I am full of sin. I am selfish. I don't deserve to be called your child. But you have embraced me and offered me your mercy. Thank you for dying on the cross for this undeserving sinner. I love you and will work hard today to show mercy and love to everyone I meet.

CHAPTER 14

Gratitude as a Path to Peace

❧

THE HEBREW BIBLE holds up a number of heroic women figures for our edification. From Eve, the mother of all the living, to Deborah, the wise warrior-judge who governed Israel with a steady hand, to Ruth, who stood by her mother-in-law Naomi with peerless loyalty, each represents virtues that all of us are encouraged to emulate. These stalwart women, called to live extraordinary lives in difficult circumstances, stand as timeless models for us. Another such woman was Judith, an incredible figure who saved the Jewish people from the onslaught of the Assyrian army.[1] She was wise beyond her years, bold in the defense of her people, and faithful to her God. With faith and cunning, she defeated and killed one of the most fearsome warriors of the ancient world, the Assyrian general Holofernes, thus freeing Israel from the grip of foreign domination.

Yet along with her courage and wisdom, another astonishing characteristic of Judith's that often goes unnoticed is her gratitude, a virtue born of recognition of God's providential goodness in her life and the lives of her fellow Israelites. Upbraiding her countrymen for their lack of trust in God, she herself holds fast in the midst of difficulty. Even in the worst moments, Judith's faith in God and gratitude to him for his faithfulness do not flounder. Perhaps the most remarkable quality of Judith's gratitude is her ability to thank God even when his blessings are hidden from view. Most of us are thankful for the obvious gifts we receive, yet Judith takes gratitude to a whole other level, seeing even the hardships she experiences as blessings that come from the hand of a loving God. In the midst of tremendous trials with no end in sight, Judith exhorts her compatriots in the following terms:

> *In spite of everything let us give thanks to the Lord our God, who is putting us to the test as he did our ancestors. Remember what he did with Abraham, and how he tested Isaac, and what happened to Jacob in Syrian Mesopotamia, while he was tending the sheep of Laban, his mother's brother. For he has not tried us with fire, as he did them, to search their hearts, nor has he taken vengeance on us; but the Lord scourges those who are close to him in order to admonish them. (Judith 8:24–27)*

It is one of life's paradoxes that the more we have the more likely we are to complain when small things are out of place. Like spoiled children, we begin to think we deserve everything we have received freely, or at least with the help of others. Many who have suffered hardships and ordeals, on the contrary, seem more able to express gratitude when someone reaches out to them with kindness or when things suddenly take a turn for the good.

Think for a moment about a grateful soul. Think of the times you yourself have been overwhelmed with gratitude. I can think of a few, and those moments of gratitude were also the times when my soul has been most at peace. They are the moments of serenity and joy. When we ask God for the serenity to accept the things we cannot change, we are asking him to allow us to see all the good things he has already done for us and be grateful for them.

It isn't easy to be grateful. Often we simply forget to thank people for their kindness. We are busy and we take things for granted—from the meal prepared for us to our washed clothes to an email from a friend when we have been ill. Ironically, we often put much more energy into asking for favors than into giving thanks for the ones we receive. When we need something, we are capable of begging, pestering, exhorting, reminding, and promising. We can be quite ingenious in obtaining what we need or desire. Yet once we receive a favor, it's often easy for us to move on to the next thing with hardly a thought or a word for the one who made the favor possible.

Jesus brought out this point rather forcefully in one of his better-known healings. If you are familiar with the Gospel stories you may recall the story of Jesus curing ten lepers of their disease. They shout to him, pleading with him to do something about their situation. From a distance, they cry out, "Jesus, Master, have mercy on us!" (Luke 17:13). Feeling compassion toward them, Jesus tells them to go and show themselves to the priests, which is required for verification of their healing so that they can reenter society. And as they go they are made clean. On discovering that he is cured, one of the lepers turns back, praising God with a loud voice. He approaches Jesus, prostrates himself at his feet, and thanks him. The Gospel writer points out that this man isn't even a Jew; he's a Samaritan. Jesus responds to the good man with a touch of sadness, asking: "Were not ten made clean? But the other nine, where are they? Was none of them found to return and give praise to God except this foreigner?" (Luke 17:17–18). Then he says to the man, "Get up and go on your way; your faith has made you well."

Why, I wonder, was Jesus so sad at the lack of gratitude among the other nine men? Did he perhaps feel slighted, cheated out of the thanks that was due to him? That doesn't seem right. I think there may have been a deeper reason for Jesus's sadness. Thanksgiving makes us better people. It is a virtue of noble souls. It reveals the ability to rise out of ourselves and our self-interest to acknowledge the goodness of others. Jesus surely was saddened because he had hoped that his gift would make the lepers better men. He wanted their hearts and souls to be cleaned and healed, not just their skin. And because gratitude makes us better, it also makes us freer. To be able to forget yourself for just a moment is a first step toward a truly free spirit.

Gratitude occasionally comes naturally, especially when everything is going great in our lives. It's relatively easy to be spontaneously thankful when the sun is shining on every corner of our existence. It's another thing, however, to be thankful when things aren't so wonderful. At any given moment of our lives, you and I have a choice. We have things in our lives that are good and pleasant, and other things that are rough and difficult. We can choose to focus on the rotten things or on the good and beautiful things. Depending on which we choose, we will tend to become either embittered and angry or grateful and happy.

Imagine, for a moment, that you wake up in the morning and start thinking about the day that awaits you. You mentally run through your day's activities, with all their potential ups and downs. You also remember yesterday, with all its sad and difficult moments, as well as its beautiful and pleasant moments. Which will take priority in your thoughts? Which will dictate your mood and determine your outlook for the coming day? This isn't just a question of having a natural disposition to optimism or pessimism. Some of us do naturally look on the "bright side," while others tend to see the negative first, but beyond this natural inclination, we also choose what we will focus on.

The interesting thing is that, at least in my experience, when we choose to be thankful, we also become more confident, trusting, hopeful, and serene. Why is that? When we see the good, or at least the good side of events, we become more aware of how much in our lives is positive and how much we are loved and cared for. And this is the kind of awareness that provokes a more hopeful and trusting outlook: we realize that, even though there are things we cannot change, we are going to be okay.

We do not need to live in a pipe dream in order to become more grateful. Nor do we need to suspend disbelief or become dreamers. All we need to do is live with our feet on the ground and recognize the good things we have received.

One of the most brilliant men who ever lived, the great medieval thinker Thomas Aquinas, wrote extensively on the virtues and sought to classify them logically and systematically. He adopted the specifically Christian "theological virtues" of faith, hope, and charity, along with the classical "cardinal virtues" of prudence, justice, temperance, and fortitude, as the foundation of all the virtues. And where was thankfulness, or gratitude, in this system? Aquinas saw gratitude as a part of justice. As a virtue, Aquinas reasoned, justice disposes us to render to everyone their due, and gratitude is what is due to our benefactors. We are therefore just to them when we give them thanks. In other words, to seek out the good in our lives in order to properly thank those who have helped us is part of being just, being fair, with God and our neighbors. Being grateful is really no more than justice. The flip side, of course, is also true: when we fail to give thanks, we are in a sense being unjust toward those who have been good to us.

Perhaps the greatest truly American holiday is Thanksgiving Day.[2] Celebrated on the fourth Thursday of November, the feast day is traditionally traced back to a celebration held in Plymouth, Massachusetts, in 1621. The first official, nationwide Thanksgiving was celebrated on November 26, 1789, which President George Washington proclaimed "as a day of public thanksgiving and prayer to be observed by acknowledging with grateful hearts the many and signal favours of Almighty God."[3] Though we think of Thanksgiving primarily as a family get-together, with the beloved trappings of turkey, mashed potatoes, cranberry sauce, pumpkin pie, and an NFL football game or two, the day revolves around the idea of gratitude. We are encouraged to recognize the gifts we have received and to give thanks to our benefactors. Central to this feast is gratitude to God for his providential care of us and of our loved ones.

Climbing out from under the rubble of our lives to see the beauty that is also there is a tremendously liberating experience. The sad and difficult things in our lives threaten to submerge us in a prison of angst and self-pity. Sometimes we feel so oppressed by evil and sadness, so bound by our hardships and travails, that we lack the minimal motivation necessary to get out and do something. To be thankful is to open our eyes to beauty and to realize that there is love and goodness even behind the pain and difficulties in our lives. We matter to someone. Someone cares about us. Someone is looking out for us. Behind these gifts is a giver, and the ultimate companion, lover, and giver is God!

When you were a child, you were probably told to "count your blessings." This simple maxim conveys a great truth. When we are obliged to sit down and enumerate all the many ways in which our lives are wonderful, we are taken out of ourselves. We emerge from the prison of all the negative things that hold us down like so many shackles. Becoming grateful for what we cannot change can be a critical step toward the serenity we seek.

∞

Lord, today I promise to be more aware of my many blessings. I will find moments throughout to say "Thank you," both to you and to the people in my life who have been good to me. I will also try to thank you for the difficulties in my life. I know you have a plan to use them as well for my good.

CHAPTER 15

It's All About Joy

⚘

PERHAPS YOU SAW the acclaimed 2000 film *Chocolat,* in which the lovely Juliette Binoche played Vianne, a provocative atheist chocolatier who "liberates" a provincial French village living under the dreary pall of Christian morality. Vianne sets up a chocolate shop in the midst of Lent (of course) and teaches the townspeople how to rediscover joy by embracing temptation rather than resisting it. The implied message is that Christianity could be the greatest single obstacle to our happiness.

Christian morality seems often to be portrayed as a series of prohibitions—don't do this, don't touch that, and stay away from this other thing. This isn't just the view of Christianity in popular culture either. It often permeates our own mentality. For instance, how often have you responded, either directly or indirectly, to an invitation to have some illicit fun with, "I'd love to, but I can't. I'm a Christian." This response is similar to: "My parents won't let me." How often has faith seemed more like a curse than a blessing? Like an added weight in life rather than liberating good news? That doesn't sound like serenity of soul.

Even the Gospel message can seem severe and unbending. It is Jesus, after all, who tells his followers in no uncertain terms: "If anyone wants to become my follower, let him deny himself and take up his cross and follow me" (Matthew 16:24). When a nice young man comes to Jesus looking for moral direction, Jesus tells him: "Sell everything you own, give your money to the poor, then come follow me." And Jesus sums up his teaching on abnegation with these words: "He who wants to save his life will lose it, and he who loses his life for my sake will find it" (Matthew 16:25).

All of this sounds as if maybe the pagans have it right. Is Christianity just bad news? The strange thing is, Christianity claims to offer a message of joy. Good news. Over and over again, we are struck with this message. Remember the great Christmas proclamation?

The people who walked in darkness have seen a great light; those who lived in a land of deep darkness, on them light has shined. You have multiplied the nation, you have increased its joy; they rejoice before you as with joy at the harvest, as people exult when dividing plunder. For a child has been born for us, a son given to us; authority rests upon his shoulders; and he is named Wonderful Counselor, Mighty God, Everlasting Father, Prince of Peace. (Isaiah 9:2–3, 6)

And this is just the beginning. The Angel Gabriel greets Mary with the acclamation: "Rejoice, highly favored one, the Lord is with you!" When pregnant Mary visits Elizabeth, the baby John the Baptist leaps in Elizabeth's womb for joy. And at the birth of Christ the angels proclaim "good news of great joy for all the people." In his public life Jesus announces: "I have come that they may have life and have it to the full," and even austere Saint Paul "commands" Christians to be joyful! "Rejoice in the Lord always; again I will say, Rejoice" (Philippians 4:4). In his last instructions to the Thessalonians, Paul expresses this joy as God's will for them: "Rejoice always, pray without ceasing, give thanks in all circumstances; for this is the will of God in Christ Jesus for you" (1 Thessalonians 5:16–18).

What does all this mean for us modern-day followers of Jesus? Simply watching the nightly news is enough to feel all the joy sucked out of us, so dismal is the situation of the world in which we live. We more easily identify with the Salve Regina hymn, which speaks of "mourning and weeping in this valley of tears." Sometimes life just seems like a drag, and yet, somehow, we are supposed to accept it serenely?

We have already spoken about the peace that Jesus promised his disciples, a peace the world cannot give. Christian joy is just that. It is a gift to those who know God and hold him in their hearts. If we have that peace beyond all understanding, if spiritual joy bubbles up from within, we are able to accept many things that we cannot change.

But that's hard to swallow without some explanation. "Joy" is not the same thing as "fun" or "jollity" or "mirth" or many other lighter forms of happy feelings. Fun is wonderful, but it isn't all life has to offer. Always looking for and expecting fun becomes a childish way of living and destroys the chance to pursue some of life's most important activities. Although the deeper commitments of love, family, friendship, and career demand that we stay focused on work and responsibility, they provide a lasting satisfaction that outshines mere fun. Fun, like dessert, can never be the main course in our lives.

The greatest joy comes from knowing that we are loved, that God our Father holds us in the palm of his hand. He has everything under control, and we can rest in him. Even the Christian moral life becomes beautiful, despite its many difficulties, when we realize that God asks what he does simply out of love for us. Far from being imposed as an arbitrary burden to keep us from having fun, his precepts are offered to illuminate for us the path of true and lasting joy.

At times I have felt a bit guilty for being joyful, as if maybe I'm being insensitive to the many sufferings of other people. *What right do I have to be joyful,* I sometimes think, *when so many others are in pain?* The rock band Jethro Tull put it like this: "How can you laugh when your own mother is hungry?" Despite the good intentions behind this attitude, I know it is fundamentally wrong. It is true that there is a great deal of misery and injustice in the world, but being a "sourpuss Christian" (as Pope Francis would say) or rejecting joy, even in the name of solidarity with the suffering, does not make the world a better place. Everyone needs a reason to hope. Seeing true joy in another person allows us to believe that joy is possible and attainable. In this way, joy can even be contagious. It can spread beyond ourselves and make other people's lives just a little bit more joyful too. In my travels I have always been astounded by how much joy abounds in many of the very poorest regions. There are more smiling, happy people in the poor neighborhoods of South America, Haiti, and Africa than in many parts of affluent Europe. Despite real deprivations, people can still experience joy.

I have always been intrigued by Saint Paul's command that Christian communities practice joy. Years ago I remember asking myself: How is that possible? Isn't joy just a feeling, an emotion that comes and goes as it will? How can we be commanded to feel a certain way? I think that there is indeed a spontaneous joy that we experience without looking for it. But there is also a joy that is a choice, even a virtue. We can choose to live in joy, to give joy to others, and this seems more important now than ever. Years ago the great Swiss theologian Hans Urs von Balthasar wrote: "Amid all the fear that characterizes our time, we Christians are summoned to live in joy and communicate joy."[1] Joy is a gift we Christians are called to give to the world.

One means we have of becoming joyful is to focus on the incredible gifts we receive through our faith. To experience the ultimate victory that Christ won over death and sin is to have a reason to be joyful no matter what the circumstances in our life. Jesus compares his Kingdom to a treasure hidden in a field. He describes a person who discovers the treasure, then joyfully runs off to sell everything he owns to buy the field with the treasure in it (see Matthew 13:44–46). The man could be sad, thinking of all the things he is selling, but he is not. He is focused on his good fortune in finding a true treasure. The joy is simply overwhelming. Or think of a man who discovers the love of his life and marries her. It would be very strange if he were to sadly march down the aisle, distressed at having left behind all the other women in the world. The joy of his marriage washes away the sacrifices that his choice entails.

What holds us back from being truly joyful? Is it suffering? I don't think so. Suffering doesn't kill joy. Joy is compatible with everything except sin and a divided heart. When we give to God only a part of our heart, only a part of our lives, knowing that he wants everything, we wind up sad and frustrated. Our hearts are made to love without conditions, without limits. Generosity brings joy, while stingy half-measures do not. Think of the happiest people you know. Aren't they the most selfless and generous people you know? Joyful people are also the ones most able to accept the things they cannot change.

Here's a reminder, as we close out the first part of our journey, to continue to pray the Serenity Prayer every day, or even multiple times a day. More than intellectual understanding, we are asking God to work a miracle in our hearts, that we might become men and women of serenity, courage, and wisdom. This miracle will happen if we knock on the door of God's heart, if we beg him to give us the gift of a simple life, filled with his presence.

∞

Lord, I have nothing to complain about. You have given me life and the gift of faith. You have loved me and given your life for me. Today I let go of all those things that try to steal my joy. I reject sin and selfishness. I embrace love and simplicity. With your grace, I choose to rejoice.

PART TWO

The Courage to Change
the Things I Can

As we turn to the second part of the Serenity Prayer, I would remind you once again to be praying it every day, even several times a day, as you come along with me on this journey toward the peace and joy God wants for you. Praying the Serenity Prayer is a habit that will stay with you for life. Growing in spiritual knowledge without also growing in practical, living faith is treacherous for the soul—it has a way of dulling the conscience and hardening the heart. Have you ever had a minister or a priest who knew all the right answers and knew the Bible cover to cover, but treated people badly? It can happen to any one of us, clergy or laity. We can read piles of spiritual books, study the Bible, and go to church, but never come to a deep, personal relationship with Jesus that transforms our lives.

Pray, pray, pray. This is the way to read this book.

In looking at the three elements of the first part of the Serenity Prayer—serenity, acceptance, and acknowledgment of the things we cannot change—we have turned them over and tried to understand their practical consequences for our lives. The second part of the Serenity Prayer also has three components—courage, change, and changeable things. We will examine these in some depth, but it would help to start with a sense of what we mean by each one.

Courage, or "fortitude," is a virtue. It has been recognized as such since classical times and was considered by the ancients to be one of the four "cardinal virtues," together with prudence, justice, and temperance. To them, fortitude is "cardinal" in that it is "central," a prime virtue on which other virtues depend. We often associate courage with warriors, and there is no doubt that the battlefield is one arena where courage may shine particularly brightly. But courage, especially in our day, extends far beyond war-front trenches and battleships. It is practiced by mothers who brave difficulties and even ridicule in their daily dedication to their families, by missionaries who often preach the Gospel at great personal risk, or by young people who live by their ideals no matter what the cost.

Changing things requires the courage to abandon the comfortable status quo of our lives in order to break into the unknown of what could be. It requires sacrifice, since nothing is ever accomplished without cost. Some people relish change—like my mother, who would move from city to city every year if she could, just for the adventure of it all! Others have a hard time changing anything and instinctively bristle at any suggestion that they alter things in any way; my father, for instance, would prefer never to have moved from our first home and is happiest when he can stick with his daily routine. Sometimes, too, we may resist change because of the influence of other people—that is, some people who are important to us may not want us to change because it will adversely affect them. In this case it takes courage to continue in our endeavors without losing resolve but still maintaining a spirit of Christian charity.

Change, as we know, is neither good nor bad in itself. It has been said, simplistically, that a liberal is one for whom all change is good and a conservative is one who believes that nothing should ever be done for the first time. Neither of these stereotypes reflects the mind of the wise person who distinguishes between good change and bad change. "Improvement" is our usual term for positive change, while we call a negative change a "decline," or a step backward in the state of things. Change can mean growth or shrinking, progress or regress. A caterpillar changing into a butterfly is beautiful; a dead fish sitting for hours under the sun undergoes changes that aren't quite so pleasant. We should be eager to change all that needs changing, but suspicious of change simply for its own sake.

Making a humble commitment to changing what we can and should change requires an attitude of healthy realism. As we will see in the following chapters, accepting our real limitations while not allowing them to curb our enthusiasm is a sign of great maturity and a recipe for great fruitfulness.

CHAPTER 16

Can We Really Make a Difference?

❧

SERENE ACCEPTANCE is just part of the picture. In the Serenity Prayer, it is the first thing we ask of God, and it is vital. But it's not everything. God did not create us to be passive spectators before the world's stage. He has recruited us as his partners and given us freedom and abilities to make a difference. There may be myriad things we cannot change in life, but there are also a number of important things that we can and should change. Freedom is scary—our freedom makes us responsible for our choices, and often for our situation. But freedom is exhilarating too, because it allows us to grasp our lives in our own hands and make a difference.

We may well ask ourselves: *What's the point? Since there are so many things I cannot do, why bother doing anything at all? It will hardly make a difference.* Surveying the world's astronomic problems, we realize how foolish it is to think we can make a significant contribution. *What makes me think I can do something that others haven't done before me? How about all the times I have tried and failed?* Moreover, having put our lives trustingly in God's hands, doesn't it show a lack of trust to suddenly want to become active in our own destiny?

Do you ever avoid doing what you know you have the ability to do because you know that you will not be able to achieve perfection in it? That's a temptation. God doesn't ask of us human perfection; he asks of us commitment to do what we can.

There is an old adage, attributed to the French writer Voltaire, that "perfect is the enemy of good."[1] Insisting on perfection often results in no improvement at all. We often have to settle for doing what is possible rather than engaging only in projects that we know will bring about completely satisfactory results. In other words, doing *something* is almost always better than doing nothing at all, even when we know that we cannot do everything. It's true that we cannot solve all the world's problems. It's true that our contribution looks minuscule next to the vast needs of society. But every bit helps. In God's eyes, doing what we can is everything.

Frances Hodgson Burnett wrote a children's story called "The Land of the Blue Flower," which I first read as an adult. I found the story enchanting, and it made a deep impression on me. The story tells of a young king who is raised by a wise old man. He is brought up in virtue, surrounded by beauty and goodness, until the day he is old enough to reign over the kingdom. On that day he is brought through the streets of the city and exposed for the first time to evil and ugliness. On seeing his consternation, his nobles counsel him not to look about him, to which he replies:

> *I would not look at them if I knew that I could not help them. There is no time to look at dark things if one cannot make them brighter. I look at these because there is something to be done. I do not yet know what.*[2]

That day, as the young king walks through the alleys and side streets, seeing for himself the evil and squalor of the city, he thinks long and hard about what he can do for his people. Eventually, he issues an edict: each and every subject of his kingdom is instructed to plant a blue flower, for which the king will provide the seeds. The edict reads:

In my pleasaunce on the mountain top there grows a Blue Flower. One of my brothers, the birds, brought me its seed from an Emperor's hidden garden. It is as beautiful as the sky at dawn. It has a strange power. It dispels evil fortune and the dark thoughts which bring it. There is no time for dark thoughts—there is no time for evil. Listen to my Law. Tomorrow seeds will be given to every man, woman, and child in my kingdom—even to the newborn. Every man, woman, and child—even the newborn—is commanded by the law to plant and feed and watch over the Blue Flower. It is the work of each to make it grow. . . . You may plant by the roadside, in a cranny of a wall, in an old box or glass or tub, in any bare space in any man's field or garden. But each must plant his seeds and watch over and feed them. Next year when the Blue Flower blossoms I shall ride through my kingdom and bestow my rewards. This is my Law.

Throughout the year, the kingdom, which had grown squalid over the years, was transformed. People worked in the open air, digging in the soil. Drunkards and thieves and idlers who had never worked before came out of their dark holes and corners into the light of the sun. Scarcely any of them had ever tried to make a flower grow before, but they began thinking about it a great deal. There was less quarreling because conversations between neighbors turned always to the Blue Flower. People who were growing Blue Flowers began to keep the surrounding ground in better order. They did not like to see bits of paper and rubbish lying about, so they cleared them away. The whole land took on a new face.

The time came for the flowers to bloom, and the people shared the thrill of excitement as the first green shoots began to force their way to the surface. Then, on a splendid summer day, it was proclaimed by heralds in the streets that the king would begin his journey through the land by riding through the capital city to see the blossoming of the Blue Flowers, followed by a feast upon the plain. He walked with great pleasure through the streets, witnessing a transformed kingdom.

Then he came to a plot of land where no flower was growing. "What has happened here?" the king said. "This garden has not been neglected. It has been dug and kept free of weeds, but my Law has been broken. There is no Blue Flower." The owner of the plot, a little crippled boy, stepped trembling before the king.

"Oh King!" he cried. "I am only a cripple, and small, and I can easily be killed. I have no flowers at all. When I opened my package of seeds I was so glad that I forgot the wind was blowing, and suddenly a great gust carried them all away forever and I had not even one left. I was afraid to tell anybody."

"Go on," said the young king gently. "What did you do?"

"I could do nothing," said the little cripple. "Only I made my garden neat and kept away the weeds. And sometimes I asked other people to let me dig a little for them. And always when I went out I picked up the ugly things I saw lying about—the bits of paper and rubbish—and I dug holes for them in the earth. But I have broken your Law."

The king dismounted from his horse and lifted the little cripple up in his arms and held him against his breast. "You shall ride with me today," he said, "and go to my castle on the mountain crag and live near the stars and the sun. When you kept the weeds from your bare little garden, and when you dug for others and hid away ugliness and disorder, you planted a Blue Flower every day. You have planted more than all the rest, and your reward shall be the sweetest, for you planted without the seeds."

Like the crippled boy in this story, we have an effect on the world that will always seem small, almost insignificant, because we don't have the necessary "seeds" (talents, energy, resources, wisdom); but in God's eyes what we do with what we have is pleasing, and everything he has chosen to need from us. Immersed in the ordinariness—the meanness—of our lives, we often feel like we are doing nothing but pulling weeds from our bare little gardens, and it's natural to think that we are not being productive, that our lives are unimportant. But that's not how God sees things. He looks at the heart. He reaps spiritual fruit from our hearts rather than material fruit from our labor. He turns our weak, but genuine, effort into holy success.

When we pray for the courage to change the things we can, we are already accepting God's wonderful plan for us to be his hands and feet on this earth. Every flower that is planted and tended truly makes the world—in God's eyes—a better place. This is not a pietistic platitude to make us feel better about our limitations, but a truth we know by faith: God asks us to give only what we can because he has already committed to taking care of the rest, and our part, coupled with his, is a beautiful creation.

CHAPTER 17

Give Us This Day
Our Daily Bread for Action

✌

ETTING UP the courage to change the things we can is no easy task. Our lives are complicated, and sometimes we find ourselves in truly overwhelming circumstances.

I recently went to Rome and posted on my Facebook page and Twitter account that I would bring with me to the tomb of Saint Peter the prayer requests of followers who wished to share with me their needs. Within minutes I had received hundreds, and eventually thousands, of heartfelt pleas to ask the Lord for a miracle in their lives. A simple promise to pray for special needs elicited a more passionate response than any previous updates or tweets. The prayer requests varied from petitions for serious physical and emotional healing to the restoration of marriages to the renewal of faith in God and humanity. As I knelt before the tomb of Saint Peter, the leader of the twelve apostles, and then read all of these prayer requests on my phone, I felt some—perhaps even much—of the pain expressed to me in the messages. This pain made me pray even more fervently: "Lord, I beg of you, do not delay! These are your people. They have mustered up the courage to ask me, a sinner, to pray for them. . . . Now, please, listen to their cry."

Almost simultaneously with my urgent and somewhat desperate plea for divine mercy, I was reminded of God's usual way of providing for our needs . . . in daily doses, and alongside our own efforts. We find this method of "rationed" grace—for the good of our souls—throughout the Gospels.

In one of the most revelatory scenes in the Gospels, the disciples ask Jesus to teach them to pray (Luke 11:1–4). They know that John the Baptist has taught his disciples to pray, and now they want to hear the rest of the story from the master. Is their request at least in part an expression of their frustration at not seeing their own prayers answered? They have seen some people healed and seen others remain stuck in their infirmities. They have been eyewitnesses to Jesus's powerful miracles, but often they are stumped by difficult cases when they preach and heal in Jesus's name. They know God wants to hear their prayers, because he himself has sent them on their mission, but like ours, their results have been mixed.

Now they tell Jesus, point-blank, "Lord, teach us to pray." And Jesus gives them a straight answer: "And when you pray, say this: Our Father who art in heaven. . . ."

Every line in the Our Father is a spiritual gem, a window through which we can see straight into the heart of God. There is one line, however, that I have come to love in a special way. I mentioned it in part one in the study of acceptance and serenity, and it fits too into our present study of courage: "Give us this day our daily bread."

Daily bread. Those of us raised on Wonder bread might have a hard time with this concept at first. But bread in the time of Jesus—and in most civilized countries today—is good for no more than twenty-four hours before it gets stale and hard. I learned this the hard way. When I was sent to Rome to study philosophy and theology, I was put in charge of preparing breakfast for all the seminarians. Every morning we received a delivery of fresh bread at 5:30 AM from the local bakery. Depending on how many people came to breakfast, we would sometimes have leftover bread. I quickly noticed that when the Italian cook arrived in the early morning, and before my team of seminarians arrived to help him prepare breakfast, he would throw away the previous day's bread. I didn't like the waste and assumed—rashly—that the cook was in cahoots with the baker to purchase more bread. One day I decided to hide the leftover bread in a pantry and serve it the next day. Needless to say, I didn't last long on the job. Although the bread looked fine when I served it, nobody could eat it. It was stale. It was hard. It was yesterday's bread.

In the Our Father, Jesus tells us to ask God for our daily bread. While I often find myself asking God to work things out for me all at once, and far in advance, or whining to him about yesterday's trials, that's not what Jesus tells us to do. He tells us to ask God for the grace we need for today!

Applying this idea to the Serenity Prayer, when we ask for courage to change what we can, we are in fact saying, "Lord, grant me the courage I need today to do the things you want me to do today." We walk with God one day at a time, at a step-by-step pace set by the Good Shepherd himself.

Earlier I told you about my Uncle Dex. One of my spiritual heroes, he has been my mentor in the practice of "daily bread" and daily courage. Growing up, I knew him as the uncle who wasn't Catholic and, as far as I knew, wasn't anything. He was the workaholic architect who didn't go to many extended family functions. He was always pleasant and kind when we saw him, but my impression was that he was usually on his way out the door, going to work. Then the financial crisis of 2007–2008 struck, hitting the architecture industry especially hard, and in a young city like New York the older, better-paid architects, like Dex, were the first to lose their jobs. Dex was laid off in 2009 and spent the next year searching for a new job, with no luck. Frustrated and with no great prospects in New York, he and my Aunt Mary Ellen moved to Texas, where the cost of living was lower and the job market was better.

Uncle Dex's journey through unemployment was hard to watch. After a while, I stopped asking him about work. I knew how much he loved architecture, how proficient he was at his craft, and what a workhorse he was.

But as it turns out, I was seeing only one part of his journey. I know now that even before he was laid off, and all through the job-seeking period in New York, the Holy Spirit was hard at work on Dex's soul. And Dex was cooperating. So well did he cooperate with God's grace that when he came down with a serious illness shortly after they moved to Austin, he confronted it—and still does—with the nobility and strength of a saint.

One day I received a call from Aunt Mary Ellen. I was prepared to hear bad news because I knew the doctors still had not diagnosed the problem and the tiredness and pain were getting worse. Instead of offering dour news, however, she giggled and said: "Jonathan, honey, something beautiful is happening to Dex. I don't know how else to describe it other than that I think he is falling in love with God! I was always the religious one," she continued, "sort of, but now he is teaching me. It is simply beautiful."

One of the things Dex was teaching Mary Ellen, and then me, was how to live joyfully and peacefully in the moment by counting on God to give him everything he needed to be able to live with whatever came his way . . . that day.

In chapter 5, I shared with you part of a letter that Dex wrote to me explaining his experience of daily bread. I saved the end of that letter for this chapter on courage. You'll remember that Dex had learned to accept with serenity those things he could not change, first his unemployment and then his sickness, because he trusted God's providence to give him his daily bread. He felt no anxiety because he knew he didn't need more than God would provide. But then he made the leap to the next level of trust and courage.

In this part of the letter, Dex tells me that he is learning to "share" his daily bread with others, to "offer back to God," so to speak, the blessings God has given him to benefit someone else who may need them more:

One morning Mary Ellen said, "My friend needs my daily bread. Whatever it is today, I'm giving it to her."

And still with family worries about their concern for me, I told her at the end of one day, "My daily bread today is more than I need. I'm giving it to my children." We both knew the reasons why.

Our daily bread is always real for us—as real as when one of our needs is met—and as real as the suffering that is felt.

I suffered, but my family and friends suffered more. It was so clear—to both Mary Ellen and me—that God's loving gift of daily bread is to be received gratefully by us, and lovingly shared with others.

The courage to change the things we can does not require us to be heroic. Above all, that courage resides in a fearless yes to the whispers of the Holy Spirit inviting us to stop thinking of ourselves and to invest ourselves for others.

CHAPTER 18

Some Change Is Necessary

☙

CHANGE is not easy. Especially as we progress along life's journey, the ideals we had as young people easily give way to the routines of well-worn paths. We tire of our efforts and sometimes despair of them ever bearing fruit. But among all the reasons to give up on change, it is especially our mistakes that weigh on us and drag us down. Failure has a way of making us feel powerless and saps our desire to try again. Yet while it is true that our past actions are among those things we cannot change, we can learn from them and grow in ways we would otherwise never have imagined. One of the most important types of change to which we are called is known in Christian terms as "repentance." To repent is to make a change, of course, in favor of a better, more righteous life.

One of my favorite modern authors is the novelist and short story writer Flannery O'Connor. She lived only to the age of thirty-nine, but in her short time she wrote some of the best English literature of all time. Her *Complete Stories* won the National Book Award for Fiction in 1972, and in this Internet age she has become even more popular. She had a rare quality of spiritual giants: being able to seamlessly incorporate faith and reason into whatever she wrote. She was above all a writer of fiction, but you can read her short stories and come away thoroughly inspired without knowing exactly how she did it.

Like some of the great spiritual mystics who blended theology, philosophy, and asceticism without distinguishing between the three (Boethius, for example), Flannery O'Connor viewed the Christian life as uncomplicated: no matter what hand providence deals us, she believed, if we are determined to follow God's holy will, there is always a holy solution to our predicament. She could not only tell a great story but sum up for the reader—and for any follower of Jesus—the essence of the big questions of life. For example, she once said—and this is important to our discussion of courage and change—that a healthy soul has three qualities: gratitude, contrition (repentance), and mission. Think about that for a moment. Do you know anyone who is consistently grateful, contrite, and living in a state of service who isn't also happy and holy? In fact, these are the kind of people we love to be with. They are always thinking about others and are fully satisfied themselves.

Repentance is a healthy psychological and spiritual exercise. I think Sigmund Freud was mistaken in assigning such a negative role to guilt feelings. He believed that guilt arises from a conflict between the overbearing superego (a sort of parental imprint) and the id (the seat of instinctual desires). According to Freud, the superego and the guilt that comes from it irrationally hold back the individual from true freedom. In reality, guilt feelings, when measured and balanced, play an important role in our psychological health. In coming to grips with the consequences of our decisions, we are motivated to change what needs changing. Covering up our faults gets us nowhere and closes the door to the conversion we all need.

To weep for sorrow at our mistakes, especially those that have hurt other people, is healthy and purifying. It is right to feel remorse for our wrongdoings. Only sociopaths feel no regret for the pain and damage they cause others. Yet the purpose of this sorrow is not to place us forever in a state of distress and anguish, but rather to move us to hate our sins, to disassociate ourselves from them, and to disown them. "Conversion" literally means a "turning toward," or a change in orientation. Conversion is what happens when we turn away from sin and turn instead toward God.

Because the enemy of our soul—the devil—is the father of lies, he is a master at turning a healthy feeling like guilt into a destructive force if we aren't careful. If your guilty feelings persist long after you have asked God for forgiveness, those feelings are no longer from God. They are, rather, signs of self-pity and distrust in the Lord's mercy. Scrupulosity—seeing sin where there is none and feeling guilty for things that are not wrong at all—is another lie that the devil loves to tell.

The devil is intent on reversing the nature of repentance because he knows that it is such a beautiful, godly act. He knows that a contrite heart is a humble heart and that the humble man or woman is close to the heart of Jesus.

How do we form a contrite heart? As just mentioned, it involves a "turning," as well as an act of the will not to do again what we have done wrong. We also ask forgiveness of those whom we have hurt and betrayed. But whether our sin has hurt others or is solely personal, we must start by asking forgiveness of God for having abused the gift of free will for selfish purposes. He alone is capable of truly removing our guilt and making us completely whole again.

One of the most famous conversion stories of all time is that of Saint Augustine, a bishop who lived in the north of Africa in the fourth century. We know about it thanks to a fascinating book he wrote detailing the long and beautiful process of accepting God in his life. If you haven't read his *Confessions,* I heartily recommend it. Despite the title, the book isn't a series of salacious stories, like some tell-all memoirs, but rather a grateful recounting of God's mercy and his triumph in Augustine's life. We can readily identify with Augustine's resistance to change. He had become attached to his lifestyle and thought that a life of virtue was beyond his capabilities. So, as much as he desired it, the inertia of vice kept holding him back. As Augustine himself put it, speaking in dialogue with God:

> *When on all sides you showed me that your words were true, and I was overcome by your truth, I had no answer whatsoever to make, but only those slow and drowsy words, "Right away. Yes, right away." "Let me be for a little while." But "Right away—right away" was never right now, and "Let me be for a little while" stretched out for a long time.*[1]

I have always found Augustine's "humanity" very consoling and encouraging. When he describes his lethargy in embracing the difficult things God asks of him, I can identify with him completely. But I also think to myself: *If he could do it, why can't I?* And why can't you?

Conversion begins with a recognition of our mistakes, continues with a plea for forgiveness, and moves on to an acceptance of the gift of forgiveness and cooperation with God's grace in beginning again. Forgiveness can be awfully hard to bestow, but sometimes it is also hard to accept. It is tough to believe that we are truly forgiven, and tough to forgive ourselves as well. This whole notion of "forgiving oneself" is often misunderstood, as if we could somehow remove our own guilt. We cannot. To forgive ourselves in any real sense can only mean to open ourselves to the forgiveness freely given by another. This is necessary, because too often we cling to our sins, refusing to release them even though pardon has been given. We sometimes feel an unhealthy psychological need to keep beating ourselves up over past failings that have already been washed away. Learning from our failings is one thing; wallowing in our unworthiness is another.

We often think of conversion as a monumental, life-changing moment that marks us forever. For some people, I suppose it is. But that isn't the only sort of conversion. Most people don't have a dramatic conversion experience (like Augustine's!), but all of us are called to daily conversion. We are called to reorder our lives each and every day of our existence. Saint John the Evangelist wrote: "If we say we have no sin in us, we are deceiving ourselves and refusing to admit the truth" (1 John 1:8). Despite our basic orientation toward God, each day we need to turn back to him anew. Every day we need to choose him again as the Lord of our lives.

Back in 1984, Pope John Paul II wrote a letter about conversion in which he summed up the idea of penance and conversion in the following terms:

> The concrete daily effort of a person, supported by God's grace, to lose his or her own life for Christ as the only means of gaining it; an effort to put off the old man and put on the new; an effort to overcome in oneself what is of the flesh in order that what is spiritual may prevail; a continual effort to rise from the things of here below to the things of above, where Christ is.[2]

What a beautiful description of the path to changing what can and must be changed in our lives! In this sense, conversion is our daily effort to be the sort of person God wants us to be—a joyful convert. The saints, then, are really just courageous sinners, people like you and me, who are unafraid to change because they depend daily on God's sufficient grace.

∞

Lord, give me the courage to change the things about myself that need changing. I cannot do this alone, but only with your help. Please forgive me for my past mistakes and help me to rebuild my life according to your plan for me. Take me by the hand and lead me where you want me to go.

CHAPTER 19

Who Is Courageous Anymore?

ॐ

I N THE ANCIENT WORLD, people would vie with each other on the battlefield or in the arena to prove their courage, which was considered one of the most important virtues a person could possess. Nowadays we speak less of this particular quality. We have replaced it with other virtues that seem more important for our times, like tolerance, fairness, open-mindedness, and ecological awareness. These are certainly all virtues, properly understood, but courage seems to have been lost in the shuffle, and this is a pity.

Doing the right thing is never easy, and we need courage in modern times no less than we did in ages past. There are now more shortcuts in our lives, and certainly we experience less physical pain, thanks to everything from aspirin to air conditioning to Novocain, but just because our lives are easier in some ways doesn't mean that courage has no place. For instance, with less healthy sacrifice built into our lives than in generations past, it may take more courage today to hold a marriage together. Perhaps it takes more courage to stand against the tide of popular opinion and speak out for the truth.

Courage—or fortitude, as it was often called—is a virtue that disposes us to face challenges and not back down. And today challenges abound.

The courage to change what we can embraces an awful lot. There is a whole world out there in need of changing. There are unjust social structures, crooked politicians, starving babies, unemployed workers, lonely senior citizens, disoriented teenagers, and nonbelievers in need of faith. There is also you and me. We need changing too.

Without some willpower and perseverance, we will never attain the goals we set. Often we find ourselves in ruts that seem to engulf us. Sometimes we feel imprisoned by our own vices, patterns of behavior, and sins. It could be cigarette smoking, compulsive eating, pornography, anger, resentment, laziness, distrust, or any other form of behavior we find hard to leave behind us. We know what we should do, but no matter how many times we resolve to change we still fall back into the same shtick.

Over the last year I have had the privilege of serving in the campus ministry program of Columbia University. Unfortunately, academia in America traditionally has been one of the areas of our culture where faith in God, seen as only for the weak-minded, is mocked or derided as irrational. That's why it has been so refreshing to accompany so many Columbia University students as they live out their faith against such strong currents. When I sit with a group of students studying the Bible on a Friday night and hear them passionately and smartly discuss what Jesus meant by a parable; when I see an email from a college freshman promoting a service opportunity to the poor in our neighborhood; when I look out on a large crowd of students at our Sunday evening service during prime study hours . . . I'm humbled. Their personal commitment to God and to living according to their faith through evangelization and other forms of service, whatever the consequences, makes me want to be a better man and a more courageous minister of God.

∞

Give me courage, Lord. I need it now more than ever. Don't let me back down when I shouldn't. Don't let me walk away when I can make a difference. Don't let me settle when I could and should do better.

CHAPTER 20

You've Got a Big Part in the Play

❧

I'VE READ few books as compelling as J. R. R. Tolkien's *Lord of the Rings* trilogy. For Tolkien, his stories weren't just stories. *The Lord of the Rings* is an epic allegory of human existence and the eternal struggle between good and evil, packed with meaning and life lessons. Tolkien, a devout Catholic, had a deeply Christian understanding of the world, which was reflected in his writing. A key theme that emerges from *The Hobbit* and *The Lord of the Rings* is the importance of what the world considers unimportant. The heroes of the story are not the great men, or the immortal elves, or the stalwart dwarves, or even the sage and powerful wizard. The heroes are the hobbits, or "halflings," the small, comfort-loving, pipe-smoking country folk who know they don't count much in the great affairs of the world. They continually surprise us because no one expects much from them. Perhaps most of all, they surprise themselves.

It's easy to think that the world is changed by other people. Who am I, after all, and who are you? If this question reflects true humility—if in asking it we are recognizing that without

God's grace we can do nothing—then it's a good thing. We have all known people who think that the world revolves around them, and they tend to be the most disagreeable of companions. Still, we should never underestimate what God intends to do, and is perfectly capable of doing, through us. Throughout history, most of the truly great men and women never considered themselves particularly special. Sometimes it was mere circumstance that moved them to show the quality of their character.

The Anglican theologian and convert Cardinal John Henry Newman was one of these great men. Besides being a stellar academic, Newman was a deeply prayerful and pious man, and his written prayers were an important addition to the great treasury of the Church's devotions. One that I find particularly moving is a meditation he wrote in 1848, when he was feeling unsure of himself and unclear about his path. It expressed great confidence in God's providence and a deep sense of peace just in knowing that God was in charge. But it also embraced the commitment that God was asking of him.

Newman begins his meditation with these words: "I am created to do something or to be something for which no one else is created; I have a place in God's counsels, in God's world, which no one else has; whether I be rich or poor, despised or esteemed by man, God knows me and calls me by my name."[1] Wow! What an amazing thought. This profound statement was true not just for Newman—it is true for each one of us. I find that it helps me to repeat it over and over. We have a unique place in God's heart and a unique part in his plan for the world and human history. None of us is an accident of birth, a chance meeting of gametes. No matter what our circumstances, we are here because God wanted us here, and still does. We believe by faith but also by overwhelming evidence that what makes us who we are is our soul. It's the constitutive, divine quality of our being. This is true of every human being, regardless of how they were conceived, whether by a loving act of spousal unity or by fleeting lust or even by sexual violence—God made every one of us. In an instant full of love, he breathed into the matter that would become our bodies an eternal soul that he willed, loved, and made part of his plan.

So Newman continues his reflection: "God has created me to do Him some definite service; He has committed some work to me which He has not committed to another. I have my mission—I never may know it in this life, but I shall be told it in the next. Somehow I am necessary for His purposes, as necessary in my place as an Archangel in his." That is a stunning declaration for a man who was never given to hyperbole. No matter who you are, or how humble your life may seem, your life is critically important to God. Who is to say that your role in history is less important than the president's or the pope's? God needs you because he has chosen to need you. Your part is yours alone, and you are irreplaceable.

To understand this, we cannot judge ourselves or others from outward appearances. We must put ourselves on another plane. You no doubt recall that beautiful line from scripture: "Not as man sees does God see, for man sees appearances, while God looks into the heart" (1 Samuel 16:7).

So if our role is so important, one of life's principal tasks is to find out what that role is. The funny thing is, God rarely reveals it all at once. Our role unfolds like chapters in a novel, with all sorts of unexpected plot twists. Just when we think we have our mission all figured out, God throws us a curveball and we find ourselves scratching our heads, wondering again what he wants from us. He sees the big picture, while we see only little bits and pieces. Newman describes it this way: "I have a part in this great work; I am a link in a chain, a bond of connection between persons. He has not created me for naught. I shall do good, I shall do His work; I shall be an angel of peace, a preacher of truth in my own place, while not intending it, if I do but keep His commandments and serve Him in my calling."

Sometimes just doing what we are supposed to be doing is the surest way of fulfilling our mission. Getting up, feeding the kids, going to work, visiting a friend, writing an email, making time for prayer, cleaning the house . . . so many seemingly mundane things are the fabric of a mission that God considers precious. We cannot calculate the effects of our actions or the importance of our choices. Only God sees all.

Newman concludes his meditation by throwing himself into God's hands, like Jesus on the cross, commending his spirit to God. "Therefore I will trust Him," Newman writes.

Whatever, wherever I am, I can never be thrown away. If I am in sickness, my sickness may serve Him; in perplexity, my perplexity may serve Him; if I am in sorrow, my sorrow may serve Him. My sickness, or perplexity, or sorrow may be necessary causes of some great end, which is quite beyond us. He does nothing in vain; He may prolong my life, He may shorten it; He knows what He is about. He may take away my friends, He may throw me among strangers, He may make me feel desolate, make my spirits sink, hide the future from me—still He knows what He is about.

What a great consolation to think that God is bringing good—right now, right this minute—out of the rubble of my life. There is nothing that is useless about my existence. My sickness, my sadness, my ups and downs, my failures . . . everything is important to him. He is the one who makes all things new.

The courage to change what we can depends on our understanding of how important our lives are. We are called to greatness—God's sort of greatness—and never should we think that our lives don't matter in the big picture of human history. They matter far more than we realize.

∞

Lord, as big or as small as my lifework may appear in the eyes of the world, I trust that it is all-important to you. I renew my commitment today to be courageous against all odds. I will not give in to the fear of failure. I will do what I know I should do. I will live my part in your grand novel even as I pray that you reveal to me what this role is. And I will trust you for the rest.

CHAPTER 21

In God's Eyes,
We Are All Action Figures

❧

HAVE YOU EVER noticed how many of Jesus's parables have to do with getting out and doing something—and how displeased he seems when we fail to act? Think, for example, of the parable of the talents (see Matthew 25:14–30 or Luke 19:11–26). In essence, it is a parable about a master or a king who entrusts his property to servants, hoping that they will know how to make something of it. When the master returns, he is visibly content with the servants who multiplied what they had been given and only becomes angry with the last servant, who decided to bury his talent rather than invest it. Note well that this fellow didn't squander what he had been given. He didn't spend it or lose it. In fact, he very carefully preserved it so the master would still have it upon his return. Yet this isn't good enough. The master expects more of him. The lesson—at least one of them—is clear. God entrusts us with his gifts and intends for us to act. Keeping the faith is not good enough. We are called to spread it.

Or think of Jesus's parable of the last judgment, the time when he will gather all peoples before him and separate them as a shepherd separates sheep from goats (Matthew 25:31–46). What I find bizarre about this parable is that the condemned folks—the goats—are not charged with any of the crimes that you and I associate with really bad behavior. Jesus doesn't say, "Away from me, you horrible thieves, adulterers, rapists, and murderers." In fact, he doesn't mention a single thing they have done wrong! Their crime was their inaction, not their action. "Away from me," he says, "for I was hungry and you gave me no food; I was thirsty and you gave me no drink, naked and you didn't clothe me, sick and in prison and you didn't visit me." They had a job to do and didn't do it. There were good actions they were expected to perform, and they failed to perform them.

The examples go on and on, and the message is very evident. God created us to do good and not just avoid evil. He wants us as coworkers rather than idle spectators. As Jesus says at one point, "Whoever does not gather with me scatters" (Luke 11:23). Doing good is, in essence, the meaning of Christianity. In the Acts of the Apostles, Saint Peter sums up Jesus's public ministry by simply saying that he "went about doing good" (Acts 10:38). To be a Christian is to be assigned a mission. It means infinitely more than simply avoiding evil. "Doing nothing wrong" no more explains the meaning of Christian life than "getting no penalties" sums up the purpose of a football game. A player who thinks he's playing well simply because he has eluded penalties but who has made no positive contribution to the team will soon find himself warming the bench.

Thomas Aquinas calls this sort of passivity—this failure to act when we are called to act—"sins of omission." At the beginning of every Catholic liturgy we pray an "act of contrition."

We ask pardon for having sinned "in my thoughts and in my words, in what I have done and in what I have failed to do." We beg forgiveness not only for the bad deeds we have done but also for the good things we have failed to do—the opportunities wasted, the inspirations ignored, or the assistance we didn't give to those in need. Since our Christian mission is to go out and transform the world with the message of the Gospel and the practice of Christian love, we would be remiss if our days and weeks were to pass by without actively engaging in this mission. A clear conscience is one that is contributing to the mission of Christ and his people.

So a truly Christian examination of conscience wouldn't merely ask: Have I done anything wrong? It would also ask: How have I witnessed to my faith? How have I lived out Christian charity? How much time have I devoted to others' needs rather than my own?

In a fascinating text that Saint John Paul II wrote back in 1981, he exhorts Christians to become active in changing the world. With the zeal of a prophet, John Paul writes that a new state of affairs today, both in the Church and in the world, "calls with a particular urgency for the action of the lay faithful." If a lack of commitment is always unacceptable, he observes, "the present time renders it even more so. It is not permissible for anyone to remain idle."[1] Yes, we must serenely accept those things we cannot change, but we must likewise courageously change those things we can. The mission of the Church belongs to each of us. Moreover, John Paul adds, "since the work that awaits everyone in the vineyard of the Lord is so great there is no place for idleness."

The world will only become what it could be through the committed action of believers. We are not called to wait and watch what happens. A Christian is not a passive observer of world events, but an active catalyst of change. Jesus's last words to his disciples were not to hunker down and patiently wait for the second coming. He didn't tell them to find a safe place to hide where they could "keep the faith." He said rather: "Go out to the whole world and make disciples of all the nations." His last words were an enormous and daunting commission, a sending forth, and they were addressed to all of us.

Every Christian is called to evangelize. Some will preach, others will counsel, and most will bear the silent witness of their faith, their hope, and their Christian charity. There is no witness more effective than love. In his marvelous first encyclical letter, titled simply *God Is Love,* Pope Benedict XVI memorably writes that "a pure and generous love is the best witness to the God in whom we believe and by whom we are driven to love." He adds: "A Christian knows when it is time to speak of God and when it is better to say nothing and to let love alone speak. He knows that God is love and that God's presence is felt at the very time when the only thing we do is to love."[2] This is the pattern for every Christian witness, regardless of its concrete form.

The mission of the laity is immense: we are called to nothing short of the evangelization of the world—or, in Jesus's words, to "make disciples of all the nations" (Matthew 28:19). Sadly, often when a generous person inquires how he or she can become more "active" in the Church, the response is unsatisfactory and unimaginative. We always run the risk of clericalizing the laity and laicizing the clergy. Too often, when a layperson wants to become active, we immediately think no further than the Sunday liturgy and the parish council. Good things, yes, but the mere tip of the iceberg. The life of the Church extends beyond the doors of the church building and beyond Sunday morning.

The mission of the Church is to change the world. When Jesus describes his followers, he uses three images. He calls us light, salt, and leaven (yeast). Interestingly, these three images share a common thread: none of them exists for its own sake. No one stares at a lantern. No one eats a plate of salt or a leaven sandwich (except the Australians—think Vegemite). Light, salt, and leaven are items that are meant to have an effect on other items. A lantern illuminates the world around us. Salt flavors food. Leaven makes bread rise. This is their purpose: to change the world around them.

The light of the Church shines not just for an hour on Sunday morning. It must shine seven days a week. The Church in the world is the community of believers in Jesus Christ who bring their faith to bear on everything they do—in the home, in the office, in the classroom, at the mall, in the factory, at the grocery store, in the boardroom. There is an elderly woman in the parish where I work who lifts my heart every time I see her. Despite the many aches, pains, and difficulties of old age that must afflict her, all I see is her smile. And her smile makes the world—my world—a better place. It is her gift to me, and to many others. With her smile, she is an apostle of the Good News.

By our baptism we were not only cleansed of sin and welcomed into the family of God; we were also sent out as apostles to the nations. All of us are entrusted by God to share in Jesus's mission. I'm always blown away by the thought that Jesus's public ministry was only about three years long. He lived in only one place. He spoke only to a finite and relatively small number of people. Yet his message was for the whole world, for all times and places. That makes our duty of spreading his message of love and repentance all the more pressing considering that it is primarily through us that men and women today can hear the Gospel and know Christ. Wow. Jesus didn't leave the mission of evangelization just to the professionals. He entrusted it to each of us.

The Second Vatican Council, too, underscored in the strongest terms the exciting and essential role of ordinary, run-of-the-pew Catholics. "By reason of their special vocation," we read, "it belongs to the laity to seek the kingdom of God by engaging in temporal affairs and directing them according to God's will."[3] And what are "temporal affairs"? That would be civil laws, medicine, entertainment, advertising, family life, sports, construction, local politics, manufacturing, engineering, communications—in other words, virtually everything! The Council adds, "It pertains to them in a special way so to illuminate and order all temporal things with which they are closely associated that these may always be effective and grow according to Christ and may be to the glory of the Creator and Redeemer." As the *Mission Impossible* television series used to say, "That is your mission, should you choose to accept it."

∞

O Lord, I need courage to get out of the rut of being a bystander to human history. I need to be creative in pinpointing my contribution, now and in the future. Beginning today, I will keep my eyes open for every opportunity to make a positive difference in the lives of others.

CHAPTER 22

Dreamers of the World, Unite!

❧

C HANGING THE THINGS we can requires not only courage but also vision. We need to have a sense not only
of where we are but also of where we are going. When
Michelangelo, one of the greatest sculptors of all time, stood
before a huge block of marble, he didn't just start chipping away
with his chisel to see what would happen. He first would form
an idea in his mind of what he wanted the sculpture to look
like. He always had in his mind's eye the final result he was
looking for. He would make sketches and then project his idea
onto the marble, chipping away everything that was "covering
up" his masterpiece. That is where the *Pietà,* the *Moses,* and the
David came from. They existed first in Michelangelo's mind,
and then in the marble.

Changing things about ourselves or the world we live in
requires a vision, an idea of what we are looking for. We can't
simply start hacking away to see what happens. Just as Michelangelo could already "see" the finished statue in the marble
before he began sculpting it, we need to envision ourselves and
our society as they could be. Our world is the marble we are

commissioned to sculpt. As much as we need realism, which allows us to see things the way they are, we also need idealism, which allows us to see things the way they could be. Both are necessary.

Realism keeps our dreams in check, but idealism stretches us to look beyond what has been done so far in order to pursue what has yet to be accomplished. Realism is important, because it keeps us from living in a fictional world. It saves us from the disappointment of chasing after unreachable goals. But without idealism, realism takes us nowhere. Idealism challenges us to go beyond the status quo and pushes us higher and farther.

We Americans are tremendously proud of Rev. Dr. Martin Luther King Jr. (yes, "Reverend" and not just "Doctor"!) and all he accomplished for civil rights in our country. By his own admission, he was able to do this by communicating a vision to others. He could look ahead at a different sort of world, a more just and caring world, and his vision was contagious. He was able to describe it in a compelling way so that people could almost see this new world, the way he did. Despite violent opposition, his vision prevailed. All of us are familiar with that amazing speech he gave on August 28, 1963. It began with those awesome words: "I have a dream." Reverend King then painted a picture of a different world in words so articulate that when we hear them today we can still see the world he imagined.

"I have a dream," he said, "that one day on the red hills of Georgia the sons of former slaves and the sons of former slave owners will be able to sit down together at a table of brotherhood." His dream went further. He dreamed "that one day even the state of Mississippi, a desert state, sweltering with the heat of injustice and oppression, will be transformed into an oasis of freedom and justice." And his dream became even more concrete still, imagining "that my four children will one day live in a nation where they will not be judged by the color of their skin but by the content of their character." This was the legacy he left to our country.

Our dreams may not extend as far as Reverend King's. Maybe we don't have a master plan for our society. Maybe we don't see so clearly where we need to go to attain a more just and free world. But surely we can envision a better version of ourselves, a better future for our families. And this vision is essential in order to change the things we can.

Have you ever imagined your very best self? Where do you see yourself in five years? If you could change just one thing about yourself, what would it be? If your spouse, or someone close to you, could change just one thing about you, what would it be? Courageous change requires forming a vision.

∞

Heavenly Father, compared to you, I am so shortsighted. Expand my vision so that I can see myself and the world as you do. Help me to be more reflective about where I am and where I need to go. Give me the courage to form and execute a holy vision.

CHAPTER 23

The First Person to Change Is You

෧

W E WOULD ALL LIKE to change other people. We'd like our spouse to nag us less, our children to respect us more, our brothers and sisters to treat us better, our coworkers and boss to appreciate us in the ways we deserve. Moreover, we would like politicians to be both sensible and honest, and we would like wealthy people to be more generous, and we would like other drivers to be more considerate on the road. But the unhappy fact is that most of these people are outside our control. The person over whom we have the greatest influence is our own self. If we want to change someone, this is the logical place to start. "But I'm not the problem!" we say. Hmmm . . . yes and no. You and I are part of the problem. And maybe you and I could be a bigger part of the solution than we are right now.

So what should this change look like? The key is that it should make us more ourselves, not less. All change should be directed at being truly ourselves, as God made us to be. Good change is a movement toward our best selves. We spoke about vision a moment ago. Sometimes the best way to envision ourselves is to imagine how God sees us. When he looks at you, what does he see? When he dreams of you at your best, what does his dream look like? He doesn't want to force you into the mold of being somebody else. He wants to bring out the very best of who you are.

Sometimes when I appear on television I have the very unpleasant duty of wearing makeup so that my face isn't shiny or washed out by the lights, and I've learned a very important lesson from this exercise. One of the makeup artists told me one day that the key to good makeup is that it should enhance our looks, not change them. Makeup should bring out the best of our features rather than make us look like someone else. (My sisters will surely give me a hard time about this makeup analogy, but oh well!) This is, I think, what God wants from us too. Like the best "makeup artist" of the soul, God looks to enhance our character with the virtues that make us beautiful, exactly as we are.

And the soul is really where it's at. Sometimes when we think about personal improvement, our minds go instantly to superficial things. Diet and exercise probably top the list. *If only I were in better shape,* we think, *I could fit into that dress . . . have more self-confidence . . . make friends more easily.* That's fine, but are these truly the most important things?

Jesus nudges us in another direction. He says that "pagans" get all excited about food and clothing but his followers are supposed to look above and beyond these things. Material things can never be our dearest treasure or our highest priority. Saint Paul, in his letter to the Colossians, wrote: "If you have been raised with Christ, seek the things that are above, where Christ is, seated at the right hand of God. Set your minds on things that are above, not on things that are on earth" (Colossians 3:1–2). How much time do we spend "seeking the things that are above"? How much do they matter to us?

The courage to change the things we can begins with a sincere effort to change ourselves, especially our spiritual selves.

∞

Lord, I know it's easier to see the things I would like to change in others, but now you call me to change myself, and I'm ready. Show me, Lord, how you would like me to be. Give me a vision of the kind of person you created me to become. I'm ready to put in action whatever you ask of me. My heart is ready.

CHAPTER 24

Blessed Are the Merciful

❦

WE HAVE SEEN that the courage to change ourselves is not primarily about making cosmetic, exterior change. Diet and fitness goals are great, but they pale in importance next to real, internal transformation. Saint Paul reminds us that "while physical training is of some value, godliness is valuable in every way, holding promise for both the present life and the life to come" (1 Timothy 4:8). There is an internal change that is far more worthwhile than any external change we can achieve. And of all the internal changes we can pursue, none is more essential than changing our hearts. We are called to think like Christ and act like him.

What makes Christian morality unique? How is it different from that of other religions? Out of all the possible explanations, perhaps there is nothing so singular about Jesus's teaching as the centrality of mercy. Without it, quite simply, we are lost. All of us, without exception, need mercy. Mercy is a free gift that we have done nothing to earn and that we cannot live without. Yet, while mercy is "free," it does have a price. Jesus stipulates that to receive mercy we must show mercy. To receive divine forgiveness we must exhibit human forgiveness toward our fellow man.

I believe that Jesus's stipulation about mercy is not just tit-for-tat, as if he were laying out the "cost" of his mercy. I think rather that he is saying that only a merciful heart is capable of receiving God's mercy, and also, perhaps more importantly, that the one who has truly experienced God's merciful love in the depths of his soul cannot help but be merciful to others. As Jesus himself remarks when a woman known to be a sinner comes and bathes his feet with her tears, wiping them with her hair, "I tell you, her sins, which were many, have been forgiven; hence she has shown great love. But the one to whom little is forgiven, loves little" (Luke 7:47).

The Gospels bear this out at every turn. Jesus teaches his apostles to pray: "Forgive us our trespasses as we forgive those who trespass against us." He proclaims the merciful to be blessed, because they will receive mercy. He tells a compelling parable about a servant whose huge debt is pardoned by his master, but who turns on a fellow servant who owes him a small fraction of what he had owed the master (Matthew 18:21–35). All our sins and failings can be forgiven, Jesus assures us, but we must also be willing to extend the same mercy to our brothers and sisters. To learn to pardon ennobles us, making us like our Father in heaven who is rich in mercy.

The ancients held up justice as the highest human virtue and considered the "just man" to be the pinnacle of morality. Jesus doesn't take anything away from the importance of justice, but he adds to it. As he says, he didn't come to abolish the law—or the classical virtues, we might add—but to fulfill it. Justice, unless crowned by mercy, is incomplete. In one of his most beautiful teaching letters, Blessed John Paul II deals with this very question of mercy and justice. He boldly asserts that "justice alone is not enough," and that "it can even lead to the negation and destruction of itself, if that deeper power, which is love, is not allowed to shape human life in its various dimensions."[1] Mercy breaks the cycle of mutual recrimination and allows true peace to reign, beginning in our own hearts.

Think of the conflicts facing our world today. What is their root cause? I suppose there are many, but when my gaze passes over the world I see a remarkable consistency in the many strife-ridden areas that cannot seem to find peace. They seem caught in a cycle of retaliation and hatred born of suffering. *We have been hurt,* say the peoples in these regions, *so we lash out. We have been treated unjustly, so we retaliate.* Yet then the people on the other side of the conflict feel unjustly treated, so they retaliate too. And so on. When will it end? Only when someone has the generosity and the courage to say personally: *Stop! Enough! I will choose mercy.*

This is not an invitation to be weak or to abandon principles of justice. But sometimes justice simply isn't the place to start. Begin with mercy.

My biggest spiritual challenge, and blessing, over the last couple of years has been to learn how to love someone whose life choices are in public contrast to my beliefs. I'm speaking here about my dear sister Anne Marie, who a couple of years ago told the family that she had begun dating other women. It was a shock to most of us, as we knew her previous boyfriends, she had never mentioned or expressed any homosexual inclination, and she didn't fit our stereotypes of a lesbian. At first it was relatively easy to carry on as if nothing was different because she did not have a serious partner. Anne Marie came to our family gatherings, and nobody talked about that aspect of her life. She and I talked about the situation at different times privately, as did other family members, but I can't say that I knew what to say. I probably said something like, "Anne Marie, you know that I believe homosexual behavior is immoral and therefore unhealthy for your soul, so I can't encourage you in that, but I want you to know that I will always love you no matter what."

Before going further, I should say that Anne Marie has not only given me permission to write about her situation but encouraged me to speak out about what she and I are learning together about how Christian families with a member who is attracted to the same sex can learn to best love each other, how they can live mercy amid very personal and sensitive disagreements.

When I told Anne Marie that I would always love her no matter what, I didn't know how hard that would become—that is, how bad I would be at loving her—under the developing circumstances. Eventually Anne Marie started dating someone seriously and then moved to Washington, DC, where the law allowed them to marry each other. This was when it got hard for the family. None of us shared Anne Marie's conviction that she was doing the right thing. But all of us wanted to express our unconditional love for her. So did we go to the wedding or not? Did we send a card, a gift, or maybe just an email? How would we show genuine love and mercy to our sister, our daughter, our cousin, without coming across as supportive of her choice?

After the wedding, Anne Marie decided she wouldn't go to any family events where her new spouse was not welcome. There were compelling reasons, I believe, for both Anne Marie's choice and for family members' discomfort with inviting them to be at family events as a married couple. My other brothers and sisters, for example, have young children, and they did not want to be forced by Anne Marie to talk to their kids about homosexuality at this stage in their lives. They didn't want Anne Marie to introduce her spouse to their kids as their new aunt, with all of the confusion that would create. The solution I suggested initially was to tell Anne Marie not to be selfish and to just go to family events alone. I told her that sometimes you have to make a sacrifice for the sake of others. That didn't go over too well. Anne Marie explained to me that for many years she had felt like she was "acting," "living a lie," and pretending to be someone she wasn't. Now, she said, she simply couldn't do it anymore. She said that even the thought of going to a family function alone, so as not to offend anyone, made her sick to her stomach.

The dilemma reached a tipping point when all the siblings began to plan my dad's eightieth birthday party. Right from the beginning, Anne Marie said she would prefer not to be part of the planning because it would be too hard for her, knowing that she wouldn't attend under the present circumstances.

I'm telling this story because I think it is one of the most gut-wrenching and complicated—and increasingly common— moral dilemmas we find ourselves in as Christians. It serves as a case study for the bigger issue we are dealing with in this chapter of learning to love as Jesus would love when the person we are trying to love is wounded, as we all are.

In our own case, Anne Marie and my family got a miracle— not an earth-shattering miracle that made all the family pain and tension and awkwardness go away, but a miracle nonetheless. And I'm confident now that it was the first of many small miracles that will bring our family closer to each other than ever before.

Early one morning I received a text from Anne Marie asking me where she could find the full text of an interview Pope Francis had done with an Italian magazine in which Francis explained how he would deal pastorally with a homosexual person. At this early hour, we had both seen only the bold headlines, but I asked her to send me her thoughts after she finished reading the whole interview. The email I received from her later in the day told me that something beautiful, something miraculous, had happened in Anne Marie's soul. Here's part of what she wrote to me:

> *All of this to say that my first reading of the Pope's interview is that I felt like I was listening to the voice of Jesus . . . a Jesus I could believe in. I have had extreme difficulty in opening a Bible over the past number of years. I get knots in my stomach.*
>
> *Yesterday, I experienced Jesus through Francis' words. I would have been disappointed if the interview only included the substance of what was highlighted in the news cycle . . . but it didn't. It was filled with radical empathy, radical love, radical humanity while not at any point watering down the Pope's understanding of objective truth. The news clippings conveniently left out the parts about moral consequences flowing from the simple, profound, radiant message of the Gospel.*

The miracle, as I see it, is that Anne Marie experienced through Pope Francis the love of God for her in a profound way. This did not happen by a superficial reading or cherry-picking of the article to fit her beliefs. The last few sentences of the part of her email message quoted here show that she understood perfectly that the pope was not saying "anything goes." She knew he wasn't changing or denying the Church's and the Bible's teaching on homosexual sex.

So what happened? Why was Anne Marie so touched by Pope Francis's words? Why were my many attempts at explanation over the years, when I was trying to say just what he said, so insufficient and his explanation was so powerful?

After a lot of prayer and reflection, I think the difference was this: while I always focused on "speaking the truth in love" and "loving the sinner but hating the sin," Pope Francis's lead concern was communicating God's love in such a way that Anne Marie could experience it. He did this by leading with mercy without harping on the sore points that everyone already knows are based in his beliefs.

Maybe you could say this was a simple change in tone or strategy. That was my initial take. But now I believe there is much more to Francis's way than adopting a softer tone or choosing a better approach. The essential difference in his way is that he demonstrates how to love people in such a way that they can experience our love as love.

I think this was the way of Jesus. Do you remember Zacchaeus the tax collector? He was the worst of the worst in the eyes of the Jews, for he was a traitor to his own. He collected taxes from his fellow Jews to give to the Romans, and he made his money by collecting from them more than they owed. The Gospel says he was wealthy, so he must have taken a lot of money from a lot of people. We know, too, that he was short of stature and didn't care what people thought of him, for the Gospel says he "ran ahead and climbed a sycamore tree to see him, since Jesus was coming that way." A short, shameless, wealthy, curious traitor . . . not a pretty portrait! The Gospel continues: "When Jesus reached the spot, he looked up and said to him, 'Zacchaeus, come down immediately. I must stay at your house today.' So he came down at once and welcomed him gladly" (Luke 19:4–6).

What happened here? Jesus led with mercy in a way that enabled Zacchaeus to experience him for who he was. He didn't invite Zacchaeus to come down and go to the synagogue with him to read the Law of Moses about cheating and lying. He didn't give him a lecture about being a sinner. He didn't say he would eat with him only under certain conditions. He didn't make Zacchaeus go to his place. He did the exact opposite! "Zacchaeus, come down immediately. I must stay at your house today." He went to Zacchaeus's place, where he knew the tax collector would feel at home. Jesus didn't approach Zacchaeus as a preacher trying to convert him, but as Father and Friend to a broken son who needed to know he was loved. Calling him by name, Jesus even expressed how fervently, even urgently, he wanted to be with Zacchaeus: "Come down immediately. I must stay at your house today."

The most shocking and refreshing part of this story for me is that Jesus didn't feel any need to explain to the crowds why he wanted to spend time with Zacchaeus. He was even willing to risk being misunderstood by important people. The Gospel says, "All the people saw this and began to mutter, 'he has gone to be the guest of a sinner' " (Luke 19:7).

The next thing we know Zacchaeus is standing up and saying to the Lord, "Look, Lord! Here and now I give half of my possessions to the poor, and if I have cheated anybody out of anything, I will pay back four times the amount." What a conversion! Zacchaeus is now willing to go to the poorhouse for the sake of righteousness. Why? Because he has experienced that Jesus loves him!

We see the same radical empathy, radical love, and radical humanity (and divinity) in the way Jesus deals with the woman caught in adultery. Many times this parable has been quoted as proof that Jesus always dealt with sinners by reminding them of them of their sin ("go and sin no more"). I know I have done this myself.

But reread the story from the perspective of Jesus's radically different way of teaching the same truth about sin and conversion. Watch him lead with mercy.

> *The teachers of the law and the Pharisees brought in a woman caught in adultery. They made her stand before the group and said to Jesus, "Teacher, this woman was caught in the act of adultery. In the Law Moses commanded us to stone such a woman. Now what do you say?" They were using this question as a trap, in order to have a basis for accusing him. But Jesus bent down and started to write on the ground with his finger. When they kept on questioning him, he straightened up and said to them, "Let any of you who is without sin be the first to throw a stone at her." Again he stooped down and wrote on the ground. At this, those who heard began to go away one at a time, the older ones first, until only Jesus was left, with the woman still standing there. Jesus straightened up and asked her, "Woman, where are they? Has no one condemned you?" (John 8:1–11)*

Before we read the last words of Jesus to this woman, imagine what the Pharisees were saying about Jesus and his liberal ways after they left, when they met up around the corner. Since none of them were left to throw the stones, they would have had no idea what Jesus told this woman. All they knew was that he didn't stone her. He let her go. He forgave her. And because Jesus cared so much about communicating his love to this woman in a way that would let her experience it, he was willing to take some serious risks. It turns out that Jesus's actions would get him killed, including this act of apparently putting himself above the Law. He knew this would happen, but he had come to earth precisely to save the lost.

Having watched Jesus put his life on the line for her, she was now ready to hear the rest of the story of mercy—the part about repentance. When all the Pharisees had left, Jesus turned to her and said, "Then neither do I condemn you. Go now and sin no more."

Ever since my sister Anne Marie sent me the email that I shared with you earlier, God has been working powerfully in me and in other members of my family to show us how we are to love Anne Marie without giving up on our principles and beliefs. In practice, we have all felt the strong call from God to rethink how to live as a family when we disagree on sensitive, personal issues.

I don't think there is a better way to explain what God has done in us—and continues to do—than to share with you another very personal email, this one from my sister Mary Hope. She has given me permission to publish this. The only substantial change I have made to the email is to use a pseudonym for Anne Marie's partner, to protect her privacy.

Jonathan,

I think Anne Marie may have, or will be forwarding on an email I sent her earlier this week. As I had mentioned to you a couple weeks ago, Mike [Mary Hope's husband] and I really were moved by the interview by the Pope, in conjunction with Annie's email to you. I was on retreat when I saw the interview, and took the weekend to really read the interview and reflect on it. Coincidentally, Mike did the same while I was gone.

I wanted to explain a little more to you, since I didn't explain my whole reasoning to Annie, and just made it simple to her that we both decided that we needed to change our relationship with her and Sally.

From my end, it was actually a much larger process than I explained to her. That Saturday I was on retreat, the Gospel was from St. Matthew, and it was the calling of Matthew . . . the very one Francis spoke about. The priest who was doing the retreat was speaking of the significance of eating a meal with a person, and how important it is to literally share our lives with those around us, especially the "sinners" and the hurting. And he was explaining that this was not just a physical thing, but being a part of the other's life, and how important that was to reaching those who are lost.

I've been really struggling with how do you love someone completely, have them a part of your life, and not be condoning their lifestyle. Especially as an example to my kids. Our culture makes it so normal to live a gay lifestyle, or to live together before you marry, or so many things. That is all around us. I want to make sure it is clear to my children, especially through our example, that this is not a normal way of life and that this way of life will not ultimately make you happy. Up until now, it has been very clear to Mike and I that the way we should do this is to let Annie know that we love her, we would love to have her in our lives, but we cannot acknowledge their marriage and cannot have Sally and Annie together as a couple with our children around. We kind of both thought it was very simple, and were very at peace with that. We knew not everyone agreed, but we also knew we needed to do what was right for our family.

Then this all happened. When I was reading thru Pope Francis' interview it was so clear to me that I need to be immersed in my relationship with Anne Marie . . . that was the only way that she was going to experience God's love, which I feel she needs more than anything else. The pope said that no one is saved alone, as an isolated individual, but "God attracts us looking at the complex web of relationships that take place in the human community. God enters into this dynamic, this participation in the web of human relationships." Although we didn't "choose" to have this suffering in our family, it is our web that is going to ultimately make us all reach heaven. If I try to run away from that web, I'm not saying yes to the life God has asked me to live . . . even if it may be messy, confusing, and hard.

He also mentions that the church needs to heal wounds and that you can't try to fix the small issues, when you really need to heal the whole person and their wounds. Once we do this, we can talk about everything else. And to do this we need nearness and proximity. Like all of us, Anne Marie has been hurt, and I believe she is still really hurting. And, although I don't know Sally, I know that she has been hurt as well. He then talks about ministers (but I took it towards me as well) "warming the hearts of people, who walk through the dark night with them, who know how to dialogue and to descend themselves into their people's night, into the darkness, without getting lost." That hit me . . . I need to have confidence in my faith with Christ not to be afraid to be immersed into Annie's life fully. I think that was my fear for me and our family.

And lastly, Pope Francis speaks about being willing to have tension in our lives. We are never going to know clearly the answers in our lives . . . we wouldn't be growing in faith if we thought we did. I hate not knowing for sure the right thing to do, and what God wants me to do. But, I have to accept that God calls each of us slowly, and only he knows the direction he's sending us. We just have to respond, even if we don't understand the direction, and even if we don't know the end result. That I hate too!! It's scary to live this way, but we have to trust that God is leading us in the right way.

So, with that, Mike and I don't know exactly how and why, but we know we need to open our lives to Annie and Sally more, and we are ok with Sally meeting the kids. We don't know the way we will do this, and it may not be perfect. I just have to let that go, and trust that God knows.

Annie responded to our email so happy. She wants to come up here and spend the day with us and Sally. She is willing just to come and go out for dinner with Mike and me, if we aren't comfortable with them being together as a couple with the kids. I don't know what we will do, so please pray that we do it the right way. I honestly don't want to make a "big deal" about it. The older kids know that Annie is gay. And the younger ones we will be telling them that Sally is Annie's friend, and explain as needed as they get older.

I don't know where all will go from here, but I did want you to know where we are at, since I knew Annie was going to share our email with you.

Can't wait to see you next week!!

Love you lots!!

Mary Hope

As you can see, our family is still very much a work in progress. My mom and dad, my six brothers and sisters, all of us are approaching this and other situations in different ways. We are trying to be patient with each other, learn from each other, and respect the fact that God's timing for one of us is not his timing for all.

This journey of rethinking how God invites me to love has continuously brought me back to "leading with mercy" and its three outstanding characteristics: it is loving (1) without fear of being misunderstood by third parties, (2) without counting the cost, and (3) and with no personal agenda other than the good of the person I am trying to love.

The courage to change what we can means breaking down our hard-heartedness and allowing the goodness of Christ to shine in our lives, particularly by leading with mercy!

∞

Lord, I know I need mercy, because I have sinned.
I thank you for offering me mercy every day of my life.
Now I ask you for grace to be courageous in the mercy
I offer to others. I think especially of people who have
offended me, the repentant and unrepentant. I am
ready to forgive the just cause I have against them,
with your grace.

CHAPTER 25

A Bridge to Reconciliation

❦

ONE OF THE worst tortures known to man, one reserved for the worst offenders, is solitary confinement. Judy Clark, the inmate we spoke of earlier, was punished with two full years of solitary confinement when guards found the letters she wrote at the beginning of her detainment outlining her hope for escape. She described to me what solitary confinement is like and told me about the many other inmates in solitary confinement who completely lost their minds after much shorter periods. She recounted hearing inmates next to her eating their mattresses because they had completely lost touch with reality.

As social animals, human beings are meant to be with others, and we cannot bear to be alone for too long. It drives us crazy because it is in communion with other people that we are able to find ourselves. God wasn't joking when he said that it is not good for man to be alone!

As terrible as solitary confinement is, we sometimes impose a very similar punishment on ourselves. Estrangement from others is quite like solitary confinement, in that the barriers we set up between ourselves and others truly separate us from them and leave us alone within ourselves. When we have been hurt and betrayed by others, we are tempted to retreat into ourselves. We decide we can no longer trust other people or forgive the wrong we have suffered at their hands. I know people who have spent years estranged from parents or siblings with whom they fought. They will not make an overture to break down the wall between them and often rebuff others' attempts to reach out to them. Isn't this a prison? Isn't this a wall as impenetrable as a barbed-wire fence or steel bars?

Reconciliation is at the core of the Christian faith—without it, our religion would mean nothing. Jesus came to earth to be our salvation—that is, our reconciliation with God and with one another. He came as a liberator, but not to free us from external oppression or political domination, but to free us from the slavery of sin, which estranges us from God our Father and from one another. The peace he offers us comes as the fruit of this liberation.

One of the best known and most poignant parables Jesus ever told was the one that comes down to us under the name of the "Prodigal Son" (Luke 15:11–32). Through this story Jesus reveals what the heart of God is like—and especially how he longs for reconciliation and communion with his children. According to the portrait Jesus paints, the Father deeply respects the freedom of his children, even when they misuse it. He does not force us to love him. So when the younger son asks his father to advance him the share of the estate that would come to him when the father dies, the father does not hesitate to do so. He gives it to his son, knowing full well that his son will squander the inheritance that he himself has spent so many years building through hard work. And so it happens.

But the father—who has every right to be furious and resentful with his son—continues to be magnanimous. When the son comes home, worn out and hungry, the father responds unexpectedly. He doesn't reproach his son. He doesn't say, "I told you so." He doesn't even wait for the son to apologize for his terrible actions. Rather, he runs out of the house, throws his arms around his son's neck, and kisses him. His joy at having his son home overwhelms everything else. He will not even allow his son to explain himself. He sends his servants to bring a robe and a ring and sandals for his son's feet, ordering them to kill the special calf they have been fattening so they can throw a proper homecoming party for the wayward son.

What seems clear is that God cannot stand to be apart from his children. It seems to eat him up inside when we stray away from him. It isn't anger that moves him. It isn't even the pain of our willful offenses. It is his deep and enduring love for us, which shows itself especially as mercy and reconciliation. To reconcile is to rebuild a bridge that has been broken, to restore a union that has been severed. More than anything else, God's forgiveness removes the barriers that keep us separated from him and from one another.

I don't think it is mere coincidence that the older son in this same parable, the one who outwardly has behaved perfectly, the one who would never have acted like his younger, "prodigal" brother, is unable to show mercy when his brother returns.

So what does this reconciliation have to do with changing the things we can? Isn't reconciliation a free gift of God? It is indeed, but it still requires two things from us. First, we need the courage to ask for and accept God's freely given mercy. Just as the father of the Prodigal Son waited patiently for his son to return home, God will not send out a posse to force us to come home. He will embrace us when we do, but we must want to return. Second, we need the courage to extend mercy to others as well. As we have freely received, we are called to freely give. Fortunately, the more we experience the effects of God's mercy in our lives, the easier it is to bestow mercy on others.

The same inhuman experience of solitary confinement that drove some of her fellow inmates to insanity drove Judy Clark to the courageous decision to change her life. In the darkest, loneliest hours of her life, she came to accept the wrong she had done and the possibility of personal redemption, even while still behind bars. Specifically, she decided to accept the truth about the irrational and evil methods of the revolutionary group she had joined. We also have a choice. When there is distance between our heart and the heart of God or between us and another person, we can build a bridge of repentance and reconciliation.

∞

Lord, I thank you for not considering the distance between you and me too great or too small for you to be concerned with. You built a bridge of redemption for me. Now, Lord, I will try to build a bridge of mercy for those people who have offended me. Aware of the mercy you have shown to me, I now willingly let go of all resentment and bitterness toward others.

CHAPTER 26

Bearing Each Other's Crosses

❧

W HEN WE are suffering, it's very hard to see beyond our pain to the world around us. It is precisely this "getting beyond ourselves," however, that offers us the opportunity to begin to heal the wounds in our soul. When we remain aware that everyone around us has some pain to undergo—or in Christian language, has their own "cross to bear"—we grow in our communion with them, and our own sorrow becomes a vehicle for understanding theirs. This is the sense of the beautiful virtue of compassion, a word that comes from the Latin words for "suffering with" someone else. To feel compassion is to appropriate to ourselves the sorrows of others, to enter into their world and participate in it.

This virtue is exemplified by my friend Judy Clark, who has found in it a door to freedom behind bars. "Every day I interact with people whose lives are complicated, difficult, and awesome," she told me. "I sit with new mothers who have just given birth, who are at once feeling the grief of not having family with them at that momentous moment and are also overjoyed and falling in love with their incredible new babies. Sitting and listening to them; holding this new life in my arms, every time, it feels like a sacred moment that enlivens and renews me. And I feel amazed and grateful to have this opportunity, just as I feel grateful to share someone's grief and anger or try to help someone unravel the riddle of how they got themselves here. It is all very rich and meaningful and is connected to my own continuing work of repair."

Suffering can isolate us, but it can also open us to others. Lived well, it can mature us and make us more capable of nourishing others with our wisdom, peace, and understanding. This prayer attributed to Saint Francis reflects this desire and ability to nourish others through our own struggles:

> *O Divine Master,*
> *grant that I may not so much seek to be consoled,*
>   *as to console;*
> *to be understood, as to understand;*
> *to be loved, as to love.*
> *For it is in giving that we receive.*
> *It is in pardoning that we are pardoned,*
> *and it is in dying that we are born to Eternal Life.*
> *Amen.*

Francis prayed for self-forgetfulness. He prayed to be able to see and feel the needs of others above his own. He prayed for the gift of empathy. All of us tend toward selfishness. We want to be understood. We want to be listened to. We want to be respected. But our desire for all this is not more important than offering it to others. The great Catherine of Siena, whom I referred to earlier, made a pact with Jesus that I find astonishingly beautiful in its simplicity and practicality. Or rather, Jesus made a pact with her that she courageously accepted. "Catherine, you take care of my business, and I will take care of yours." That's the same pact Jesus wants to make with each of us: "Trust me to take care of you as you forget about self and live for others." The Christian faith says that selfishness is the fruit of original sin and a tendency against which we must resolutely fight. One of the first things little children learn is the idea of possession: *That's mine. Give it to me.* While this tendency comes naturally, the desire to give gifts usually does not. We need to train ourselves to think of others and to become aware of their needs, their feelings, and their well-being.

One of life's many paradoxes is that the more we focus on ourselves and our own well-being, to the neglect of our neighbor, the more unsettled and unhappy we become. When Jesus said that there is more joy to be found in giving than in receiving, he was not issuing a command that we engage in superhuman behavior. He was expounding a simple truth about human nature. The joy of giving is not a prize or reward to be given to the one who behaves correctly, but comes from the giving itself. When we love others, when we give unselfishly, we experience joy.

Selfishness is not only wrong but psychologically unhealthy. In fact, in one sense it is wrong precisely because it is unhealthy. Selfishness diminishes us and is unworthy of our dignity as human beings. Isn't it fascinating that this psychological truth is evident to some degree to everyone, believers and nonbelievers alike? Our heroes, those we admire and hold up as models, are inevitably people who live unselfish lives. People who pursue primarily their own self-interest and well-being in this life, as successful as they may be, are rarely remembered later as models, and certainly not as heroes.

The "courage to change what we can" implies the generosity to look beyond ourselves and to see the needs of others. Maybe we can't fix everything, but we can fix something. Every day presents us with opportunities to reach out, to assist someone in need, to serve. We don't change the world in one fell swoop by some sort of imperial edict. We change the world one person at a time, one act of kindness at a time.

You may have seen the charming 2007 movie *Evan Almighty*, starring Steve Carell as Evan, a modern-day Noah, and Morgan Freeman as God. God has asked Evan, to the amusement and consternation of his neighbors, friends, and family, to build an ark. Evan obediently does so, and soon his yard becomes a menagerie, filled with an array of beasts large and small. But the film ends with God telling Evan that he has misunderstood. The way to change the world, he says, is by doing one Act of Random Kindness (ARK) at a time. This is a cute Hollywood message, but it is also fundamentally true. The world is in fact changed through acts of kindness, and these are the sort of ARKs that each of us can build daily. We spend enormous amounts of time and energy—and rightly so—trying to get politics right. But no mayor, senator, Supreme Court justice, or president can do what we can do today for our neighbor.

∞

Lord, I am very well aware of my own needs and desires, but sadly, I am much less aware of the needs and desires of others. Help me to learn to put others first. Help me to break out of my selfishness in order to serve and to love, as you did. Teach me to be truly compassionate toward others. And let me experience the joy of giving rather than receiving.

CHAPTER 27

The Courage to Get Back Up
After Falling

❧

I F YOU have ever had the experience of starting something, you have probably also had the experience of failing. Even those especially gifted people who always seem to land on their feet usually have a surprising history of failed attempts. They acquire this history, however, because they were unafraid to make those attempts.

It's so easy to think that we are the unlucky ones. You probably recall the droll *Peanuts* cartoon in which, after they've lost a baseball game, Linus attempts to console Charlie Brown with the old cliché "You win some, you lose some." Charlie Brown thinks for a moment and then replies, "Gee, that would be nice."

The fact is that, however much courage is needed to climb into the ring, still more courage is needed to get back up when we have been knocked down. The courage to change the things we can is not a program for the fainthearted. Nothing worth doing is easy, and rarely do we succeed on the first try. Changing the things we can requires that we learn how to overcome not only the hurdles along the way but also the experience of our own failure.

Back in a 1993 issue of *US News & World Report,* John Leo lamented a growing campaign to remove competitive sports from schools so as to protect students from "traumas." Some well-intentioned but, in my opinion, misguided educators thought it better to put all the kids on the same team rather than engage in competitive games, which end with some kids as winners and some as losers. A healthy noncompetitive activity, according to these educators, would be for the whole class to roll a giant rubber ball around the gymnasium. As Leo persuasively argued, the success of this campaign would have been a misfortune for the country.

Sports teach the virtue of determination, "stick-to-it-iveness," teamwork, and valor. Learning to lose and learning to win, learning to get up when you've fallen, to pick up your tools and begin all over again . . . this virtue has been chiefly responsible for the greatest personal and cooperative achievements of mankind. The Duke of Wellington has been quoted as saying that "the battle of Waterloo was won on the playing fields of Eton." Learning determination also means learning to lose well. It's easy to be a good winner, but much harder to be a good loser.

Years ago a Protestant preacher friend said something that really got me thinking. He made the astonishing claim that the worst enemy of the Christian—after sin itself—is discouragement. He claimed that it is one of the favorite tools of the devil. Discouragement, he said, "breeds inaction, abdication of responsibility, and ultimately, despair." This claim, as extravagant as it seemed to me, fits with my own experience. Discouragement demotivates us. It buries us in sterile lamentation.

Nothing slows us down like discouragement. It saps our strength and enthusiasm and draws us deep into ourselves, shutting out the light and courage that the Holy Spirit gives. Especially after a fall, the devil tries to persuade us to wallow in self-pity, like a boxing coach telling his man to stay down in the ring. The devil paints everything black and makes us focus, not on God's mercy and grace, but on our own misery. He wants us to throw in the towel and give up the fight. What's the use? Who are you trying to kid? You can't do it. And yet we know God doesn't think this way. He wants us back in the fray.

The solution to discouragement is not to avoid challenges or limit our exposure. Instead, the solution is emotional and spiritual maturity, founded on the certainty that God asks of us fidelity, not success. Nor does God ask of us optimism; he asks of us realism that takes into account his grace. This vision that includes what we know by faith—that God has already won the war—allows both the natural pessimist and the natural optimist to live in the truth.

It's no fun to fall down over and over again. It's especially annoying to fall back into faults we thought we had left behind. As a result, it can be frustrating to examine our conscience when we see no progress. If we don't look at it, maybe our faults will go away. We are not alone in the temptation to discouragement. Over and over again in the Gospels, Jesus has to tell his disciples to take heart, to have courage, to not be afraid. And the Lord invites us to confidence not despite our weakness but because of it. Our poverty doesn't repel him; it moves his heart to compassion. He comes to the assistance of all who put their trust in him.

If we examine discouragement closely, we find some things that may surprise us. The first is that discouragement stems not from an excess of humility but from an excess of pride. We often have such a high opinion of ourselves that when we don't perform to the standards we set for ourselves we become disheartened. We exaggerate our own importance, as if our weakness and sins were somehow weightier than God's mercy and goodness.

Sometimes, too, discouragement emerges because we don't know ourselves very well. We have an inflated idea of ourselves and of our own virtue, so when we fall we feel surprised, confused, and ashamed and we want to give up. But here the pain comes not so much from having failed and offended God but from wounded self-love. We are embarrassed and humiliated at seeing ourselves so weak.

I see this in my own life. Because of the new world of social media, whenever I appear on television, give a homily (sermon), or write an article or book, I get tons of feedback. Some of it is positive, some of it is negative, and some of it is outright mean. When I see vicious comments on the Internet or in my mailbox from unknown people, or from people who are just angry at God or the Church, it doesn't bother me a bit. In fact, it's kind of amusing, as it teaches me about humanity and what we are capable of when we think we are anonymous. But when I get the least amount of criticism from people whom I know personally or respect from a distance and who tell me why I messed up, boy oh boy does that ever hurt. It hurts because I am proud and vain! I want to be loved and respected. I want to be wise and insightful. I want to be right. When I get hit with a particularly painful and public criticism of this sort, whether it's just or unjust, one of my reactions is to throw in the towel on such public activities. I think to myself, *Is it really worth it?* Only with time and prayer do I come to accept the fact that my discouragement comes from a wounded ego and that my ego is not the voice of God.

Putting aside discouragement and trusting in God requires that we shift our focus from our littleness to his greatness. Discouragement normally shows itself when we stop looking at God (for whom all things are possible) and become fixated on ourselves (who can do nothing without him). It can even seem that discouragement is the "proper" or "humble" response to failure, as if a cheerful confidence in God would somehow clash with the reality of our own frailty.

In these situations it is especially helpful to treat discouragement as a temptation. Feeling sorry for ourselves and allowing discouragement to get a grip on us does no one any good. It doesn't help us, it doesn't please God, and it doesn't benefit other people. In fact, the only one who comes out ahead when we are discouraged is the devil, who delights in seeing us doubt the love and mercy of God.

Think of good Peter, walking on the water, living in the midst of a miracle. The Gospel says that, "when he noticed how strong the wind was, he became afraid and started to sink" (Matthew 14:30). In other words, as soon as he took his eyes off Christ and started looking about him at the difficulties and thinking about his own human inability to do what he was in fact doing, he began to sink. Our courage and confidence come from God's strength and fidelity, not our own. It is his power that raises us up and enables us to do many things that we could never do on our own.

To overcome discouragement, two virtues are essential: courage and hope. Courage strengthens us to forge ahead despite the difficulties. We continue on without allowing our setbacks to keep us down. Hope, on the other hand, teaches us to trust in God, who will give us the grace we need to improve and who promises us ultimate victory. He never abandons us in our hour of need. He stays by our side, forgives our failings, and consoles us in our difficulties. United with him, we can truly do all things, even though progress can seem painfully slow. Someday, maybe soon, we will see our trust rewarded.

This is true not only for our worldly setbacks but for our moral and spiritual defeats as well. God never intends sin, but when we do sin he offers us his mercy immediately; he never intends for us to stay separated from him. The great saint of Auschwitz, Maximilian Kolbe, wrote: "Whenever you feel guilty, even if it is because you have consciously committed a sin, a serious sin, something you have kept doing many, many times, never let the devil deceive you by allowing him to discourage you."[1] The devil will tell us that we are losers, that God has had enough of us, that there is no hope for the likes of us. But he is the father of lies.

We need the courage to get back up and start all over again with humility and confidence. God can bring wonderful things out of our failures and falls, beginning with a greater recognition of our weaknesses and our need for his grace. Even when we have sunk very low, done very bad things, or wandered away from God for a long time, not only does hope remain an option—it is an imperative. He always calls us back to himself, always desires our friendship, and always extends his mercy to anyone who needs it. He wants us back!

∞

Dear Lord, I have done lots of bad things in my life. I rarely live up to my resolutions, and I am not the generous, loving person that you want me to be. But I believe in your love. I believe in your power to transform me. I believe that you want me to get back up and keep fighting. Prosper the work of my hands!

CHAPTER 28

Start with Baby Steps

❧

IN THE HILARIOUS 1991 motion picture *What About Bob?* Richard Dreyfuss plays a successful psychiatrist, Dr. Leo Marvin, who has to deal with the obsessive-compulsive Bob Wiley, played by Bill Murray. When he first meets Bob, Dr. Marvin doesn't feel like treating him, so he tries to quietly turn him away by giving him a copy of his new book, *Baby Steps*. His conversation with Bob goes like this:

BOB: *Baby steps.*

MARVIN: *It means setting small, reasonable goals for yourself. One day at a time, one tiny step at a time—doable, accomplishable goals.*

BOB: *Baby steps.*

MARVIN: *When you leave this office, don't think about everything you have to do to get out of the building, just deal with getting out of the room. When you reach the hall, just deal with the hall. And so forth. Baby steps.*

As crazy as this movie is, Marvin's advice isn't half bad. It sums up millennia of solid human wisdom. Turning back to our friend Aesop, we can recall his adage "Slow and steady wins the race," illustrated by the tortoise defeating the much faster hare in a race. "Rome wasn't built in a day" is a French proverb from the late 1100s about the need for patience and perseverance in our endeavors. And medieval wisdom encourages us to *age quod agis,* or "do what you're doing," an older version of living in the moment and taking it one step at a time. Often we fail in our resolutions because we don't pace ourselves. We don't measure our resources and realistically evaluate our capabilities. We bite off more than we can chew and find ourselves frustrated and angry.

Jesus, too, had a parable that makes this very point. An imprudent king is setting out with 10,000 soldiers to do battle with the 20,000 soldiers in the enemy's army (Luke 14:31–33). Don't even think about it, Jesus advises; instead, send out an envoy to sue for peace before things get ugly. And just to help the message sink in further, he also gives the example of a man who wants to build a tower but doesn't have enough resources to finish it. When he leaves the tower half built, he becomes the laughingstock of the community. Having lived in Rome for a number of years, where one sees numerous half-built bridges leading nowhere, I totally get Jesus's point. He wants us to be realists and to manage our projects with intelligence. Baby steps. Better to take on a smaller project we will complete than a more ambitious project that we'll leave half done.

So what does all this have to do with you and me? If we want to change, we need to pick small, concrete areas to work on. We're not going to change overnight. Think of all the times you have made New Year's resolutions that led nowhere. Think about the best resolutions you've made and then think about the worst ones. Look at the ones you have stuck to and those you have abandoned. It seems to me that many of our failures stem from overly ambitious programs that were made in a moment of fervor and ditched just as quickly in a moment of apathy. *What was I thinking?* we ask ourselves. The courage to change the things we can is a courage that moves forward intelligently, with persistence. Life is a marathon, not a fifty-yard dash. We are in it for the long haul, and only programs that acknowledge this are successful in the end.

∞

Lord, I know you want me to keep moving forward, even if that means doing so at a snail's pace. Help me to take small but significant steps in drawing closer to you. Help me to be satisfied with the progress you ask of me, not the progress I would like to be making.

CHAPTER 29

If David Could Do It, So Can I!

❧

I SPOKE EARLIER about King David and his problem with
Saul's armor, which turns out to be more a hindrance
than a help. We might learn quite a bit from looking a
little more closely at this great biblical figure—and be encouraged besides.

David doesn't have an awful lot going for him. You may
recall that he is a poor shepherd and the youngest in his family. In fact, when the prophet Samuel comes to his father Jesse's
house and asks Jesse to assemble his sons, Jesse doesn't even
bother to call the boy David, who is out in the fields. He is too
insignificant. Jesse assumes that anything David might be good
for, one of his older sons would be better.

But God chooses David anyway. He singles David out for
great things—to become the king of Israel. With God by his
side, David's career *begins* splendidly. Next thing you know,
David is winning battles and attracting the attention of pretty
women and garnering huge popularity. But somewhere along
the line all this starts going to his head. Soon David gets over-
confident and lazy and starts staying home when his soldiers

are on campaign. And this idleness gets him into big trouble. He spies his lovely neighbor Bathsheba bathing. She is a married woman, the wife of one of his own soldiers, Uriah. But David has gotten used to having what he wants, and he wants Bathsheba. So he takes her.

Things just keep getting worse. Bathsheba gets pregnant, and rather than come clean and admit his error, David compounds it with a much bigger one. He has his good soldier Uriah killed, by leaving him undefended in battle where the enemies are the strongest. We could go on and on about David's weaknesses and blunders. He is a tragic figure, in many ways like any of us. And yet he is a glorious figure too. Despite his sins and failings, he is humble enough, and trusts God enough, to repent. And God, being God, forgives him. Over and over, David changes what he can and lets God change the rest.

To David is attributed the authorship of one of the most beautiful psalms in the Bible. It is a psalm of deep sorrow and repentance, reputedly the one he composed after the fiasco with Bathsheba and Uriah. I won't reproduce it all here (you can find the full text in your Bible), but it begins like this: "Have mercy on me, O God, according to your steadfast love; according to your abundant mercy blot out my transgressions. Wash me thoroughly from my iniquity, and cleanse me from my sin" (Psalm 51:1–2).

History—especially salvation history—gives us example after example of weak human beings who end up doing great and important things. It's nice to know that we aren't alone in our weakness. Part of having the courage to change the things we can is refusing to make excuses for ourselves. It's much better to reach the finish line bruised and bloody than never to get in the race at all.

∞

Dear Lord, when I look at all that you are asking of me, I really don't feel very courageous. I am deeply aware of my weaknesses. Thank you for giving me so many good examples of people who were weak like me and yet overcame their weaknesses by your grace. Make me one of them!

PART THREE

The Wisdom to Know the Difference

WHEN I told friends I wanted to write a book on the Serenity Prayer and reminded them of the three parts to it, almost without exception they told me that the third part was the toughest for them. Sometimes we are able to accept peacefully difficult situations and move beyond them, they said, and sometimes we act courageously and change things we know need changing. So in a sense, they reasoned, we know about acceptance and courage, even if we don't always act courageously or feel very serene. But do we know how to be wise? Few people would be able to say yes.

So how do we learn wisdom? The good news is that for those of us who have already begun to put the first two parts of the Serenity Prayer into practice, the wisdom to know the difference between what we can change and what we cannot usually follows, whatever our level of wisdom before we began our journey. Yes, we need to learn, become discerning, and develop clarity of mind, mental discipline, and freedom from personal bias, but as we learn to accept those things we already have a hunch we can't or shouldn't change and begin to change the things we are pretty sure we can, the gray area shrinks. In other words, when we get in the habit of seeking God and obeying our conscience, we quickly find that we already have more wisdom than we might imagine!

Many years ago I found myself in the unpleasant situation of dealing with a difficult coworker. At the height of the tension I was ready to ask my superiors for a change in assignment. That only added to the stress because in fact I was very happy where I was . . . except for the presence of this coworker. I was regularly losing sleep over the thought of dealing with him the next day. I was convinced that this coworker was never going to change or leave and that I would never be able to work peacefully as long as he was around. My spiritual director (and mentor) knew the situation and usually just listened to me complain, his lack of comment implying that this was not a big deal. When I talked with him for over an hour one evening without complaining about my coworker, he asked me at the end of our session how that situation was going. "Basically the same," I said, "but there is nothing I can do."

"Are you sure?" he replied.

"He just seems to be getting worse." Then I gave him a few examples.

"But have you ever thought about spending more time with him outside of work?" As soon as I heard those terrifying words I knew this was the way forward. I think my spiritual director saw the dread on my face when I instantly realized that he was right on the money. "That's exactly what I should do," I said, "and I've known it all along."

I really had known it all along. I'd known that I needed to spend time outside of work with this coworker, but I hadn't wanted to know it. I knew this man acted like he did because he was insecure and looking for friendship and companionship. I just didn't have the courage to do it. I hated the thought of doing this very simple thing, even though I already knew it was the solution. I was too hardheaded to heed my own wisdom. It wasn't until I heard from a trusted source what I already knew to be true that I was able to convince myself to do what was right.

The wisdom to know the difference between what we can change and what we cannot has to do with discerning God's will for how we should react to a present challenge. Discernment, in this sense, is the process of discovering God's plan for us both in the big things (like who we will marry) and in our daily choices (such as whether to leave work early to go to our son's baseball game or stay and make the boss happy). The wisdom we are asking for in the Serenity Prayer is the spiritual art of discernment.

To strive with all our might to change what cannot be changed is a dreadful exercise in futility and only leads to fatigue, frustration, and despair. Such an effort is a waste of both time and energy, it causes great exasperation, and with discernment we are able to say, *This is not wise!* Fighting to move what cannot be moved, to undo what cannot be undone, saps our strength and discourages us even in our more fruitful pursuits. After such disappointment, we simply want to throw in the towel and curl up on our couches. But when we have this spiritual discernment—this applied wisdom—we spend our energy wisely, leaving aside what is without remedy and focusing on areas where we can make true progress!

Wisdom also saves us from the opposing error—passively accepting the status quo when it can and should be changed. Wisdom helps us see through the temptation to think that all our effort would be in vain when in fact effort is exactly what is needed. Wisdom unmasks our own prejudices and negative inclinations.

Perhaps it is laziness that keeps us from engaging the mission before us. Perhaps it is fear of failure that binds us to our apathy and blocks our resolve. Wisdom sees what is—it "knows" the difference.

So we pray for this as well. We pray that our good God and Father will give us the gift of wisdom—one of the precious gifts of his Holy Spirit. We are committed to working for it, but we know that we are going nowhere without him, so we humbly and confidently pray.

CHAPTER 30

Seek After Wisdom, Not Knowledge

❧

ARE YOU still praying the Serenity Prayer every day? Don't stop now! You are working to form a soul at peace, capable of instinctively letting go of the things you cannot change and tackling with courage and confidence the things you can. This prayer habit is particularly important as you move through this third section because growing in wisdom is less tangible than letting go of control, or of doing courageously what you know you should do.

Wisdom is a subtle, almost imperceptible gift from God that he gives us when we ask him for it. "Lord, grant me the wisdom to know when and how I should act and when I should let go!" That's a prayer for everyday living.

We have probably all thought about what we would do if we won the lottery. Similarly, as a kid, I remember quizzing my friends about what they would ask for if a genie were to appear to us and offer us three wishes. After they hemmed and hawed, I would offer the snarky solution of wishing for one thousand more wishes. As childish as it sounds, the quandary of deciding what to do with three wishes that would come true is actually quite fascinating. It's even more revealing than what we would do with big lottery winnings. It makes us identify our greatest unfulfilled desire: Is it money? Health? A better job? A happier marriage?

In the Old Testament we read of a scenario very similar to this. No genie comes out of a lamp, of course, but one day God does offer King Solomon the chance of a lifetime. Solomon has just been made king of Israel to succeed his father David. He is young and somewhat overwhelmed, but God gives him the chance to make a request, to ask for anything he wants. He appeared to Solomon in a dream and bids him to ask for whatever he needs. Solomon doesn't waste any time answering, and God is thrilled with Solomon's response. He does not ask for riches, or a long life, or victory over all his enemies. He asks instead for wisdom. "Give your servant," Solomon says, "an understanding mind to govern your people, able to discern between good and evil" (1 Kings 3:9). God is pleased to grant Solomon this request, and he becomes known far and wide for his wisdom. "He was wiser," we read, "than anyone else, wiser than Ethan the Ezrahite, and Heman, Calcol, and Darda, children of Mahol; his fame spread throughout all the surrounding nations" (1 Kings 4:31). Though we don't know who Ethan or Darda were, obviously they were revered by people of the time as especially wise. But Solomon was wiser still.

Today Solomon's wish might seem bizarre to us. Of all the things we might ask for, I doubt that wisdom would fall even in the top ten for most of us—perhaps because we don't hear much about the value of wisdom nowadays. We do care a great deal about knowledge and data. We are delighted that we can call up virtually any scrap of information on our smart phones at any time. We have—literally at our fingertips—more data than previous generations even dreamed of. This surfeit of information makes us smart and maybe even a little smug. We know so much more than our ancestors, who thought the world was flat, didn't know what genes or chromosomes were, and couldn't split atoms or cure pneumonia. Yet, as good as this knowledge can be, I wonder how often it translates into wisdom.

Wisdom and knowledge aren't the same thing. Wisdom is not really about knowing many things, but rather knowing (discerning) what is important. Someone can be well informed but foolish. Like a forty-niner panning for gold, wisdom sifts through the "sand" of ready information to find a treasure. In this last section of the Serenity Prayer, we ask God for "the wisdom to know the difference." We ask to be able to discern, to sort things out. We do not ask to know many more things, but to know what really matters.

Have you noticed that wise people are humble people? They know how much they don't know. They also know how little they truly need. We have many desires but relatively few true needs. In fact, the more unfulfilled desires for unnecessary things we have, the unhappier we often become. The more content we are with what we have, the more peace there is in our souls. This, too, is wisdom.

Thomas Aquinas, in his famous *Summa Theologiae,* dedicates much space to speaking of the virtues. Years ago, in reading through this, I came upon something fascinating. In two consecutive articles of this work, Aquinas discusses two habits: *studiositas* (studiousness) and *curiositas* (curiosity). What struck me as odd was Aquinas's declaration that *studiositas* is a virtue and *curiositas* is a vice. At first that seemed contradictory to me, since they share so many similarities. Both have to do with a desire to know and a will to learn. Isn't it curiosity that impels us to study? Nevertheless, Aquinas says that while *studiositas* moves us to delve into important questions and to pursue wisdom, *curiositas* encourages a sort of intellectual dilettantism and a preference for knowing many things rather than important things. A curious person skims headlines; a studious person wants to know more. Today, we don't just need well-informed men and women—we need wise men and women. Wisdom means the ability to discern between what is important and what is unimportant.

Ask yourself: In an average week, do you spend more time reading *People* magazine or your Bible? Do you know more about *American Idol* than you do about world history? We may be very well versed in all sorts of useless trivia, yet know next to nothing about the things that count. Wisdom, in fact, seems more about asking the right questions than getting all the right answers. To wonder about life's bigger issues, to spend time investigating what things really mean and why they matter, is worth more than amassing an immense store of useless factoids.

Our prayerful request for "the wisdom to know the difference" suggests that we already understand how important wisdom is, and that seems like a really good place to start. In a sense, asking for wisdom already implies a certain wisdom. That is an encouraging thought.

CHAPTER 31

Cultivating Our Interior Life

❦

INMATE Judy Clark was raised in the tradition of secular Judaism, but in recent years she has immersed herself in religious studies and clinical pastoral education and has just completed certification as a chaplain. This training lends a framework to her ongoing role as a mentor and confidante to women like herself who are serving lengthy sentences and trying to come to terms with their past and to lead compassionate, fulfilling, and productive lives.

Judy discovered something the hard way: humans need silence in order to reflect—both interior and exterior silence. Activism can be an escape from the reality of our lives. It protects us from having to face our own demons and come to grips with ourselves and our choices. When Judy was thrown into prison, and even more so when she ended up in solitary confinement, she was forced to face herself. There was no music to drown out her thoughts. There was no television or Internet to distract her from her situation. She was totally alone, with nothing to entertain or sidetrack her, and she took advantage of this situation to delve deeper into herself and to become a more spiritual person.

Judy would not have expressed it this way at the time. "I did not say," she says now, "'I'm on a spiritual journey.' It was a choice to begin to become a person and to take responsibility for my choices. Now I can recognize the spiritual aspects of my questions and my methods. When I got out of solitary housing unit (SHU), I decided that I wanted to go to Jewish services. Not primarily because I wanted to become religious, but because as I started to say, 'Who am I?' one of the things that felt intrinsic was my Jewish identity."

Forced to look inward at herself and come to grips with her identity, Judy became a more spiritual person. She became a more thoughtful person. She became a more centered person. Such interior silence is the beginning of what spiritual giants have called "the interior life," the life of grace in which we enjoy friendship with God. It is in interior silence and friendship with God that wisdom flourishes, for the closer we are to God the more easily we discern his plan for our lives.

The great philosopher Socrates claimed that the unexamined life is not worth living.[1] There is much wisdom in this simple saying. To run our daily course like a hamster furiously speeding along on its wheel and getting nowhere is to live an inhuman existence. We are called to something higher. We are called to reflect, to contemplate, to examine, to explore, and to consider. Yet nowadays we always seem to have something more important to do than simply to think about our lives— where we are going, how we are living, what sort of people we are trying to be. We run from work to the grocery store, then off to the gym, then on to that party, only to come home and immediately check our email and fall asleep to the sound of the television droning in the background. If this kind of day happened only now and then, we wouldn't be in such trouble. Our being could bear it. But for many of us this frenetic pace is frighteningly close to being "the story of our lives."

We cannot find ourselves outside ourselves. And we cannot find the fullness of wisdom outside of God. Who we are is not defined solely by what we do, and still less by what we think we have accomplished. Personal identity and integrity come from within, not from without.

In 1952 the German scholar Josef Pieper wrote a provocative little book titled *Leisure: The Basis of Culture.* He argues convincingly that true culture is the fruit of our "downtime," when we stop the frenetic pace of our labors and devote ourselves to pursuits that are not immediately "productive." Work, Pieper says, is ordered to leisure, not the other way around. In the Western world, most of us think of leisure as mere idleness or wasted time; by contrast, Pieper contends that leisure ultimately is dedication to higher things (not lower). In fact, our common sense tells us that only when we have a moment to breathe and step back from the rat race can we truly start thinking about what we are about and why we do what we do.

This doesn't mean that all leisure is equally beneficial to our deeper selves. Pieper would have recoiled at the idea, for instance, that leisure consists of video games and passive television watching. Laziness and idleness lead to boredom and keep us from properly enjoying leisure. While leisure, by definition, is a break from work, not all leisure builds the soul or makes us better people.

If you are taking the time to read this book, you probably already know this, or at least sense it, and are doing something about it. Reading forces us to think, to grapple with ideas and concepts, and inevitably to examine our lives and choices. It challenges our minds and souls. To be spiritual means, in the first place, to recognize and pursue an interior dimension to being human. It means taking a step back to consider and reflect—on the present, the past, and the future. It means asking the bigger questions about life and its purpose. To be spiritual, in fact, is to already be searching for "the wisdom to know the difference."

CHAPTER 32

Spiritual but Not Religious?

એ

No DOUBT you have heard people say they are "spiritual but not religious." What many people mean when they say this is that they are seeking a happy medium between crass materialism and fanatical zealotry. But when it requires no specific commitment, sometimes "being spiritual" can be a cop-out. After all, the fact that we are spiritual—that we have a soul—is a pure gift from God. We all have a soul. That's not a virtue or quality of our own making. Religion, on the other hand, is man's expression of his spirituality. Whether it takes the form of participating in liturgy within a church or getting down on one's knees before going to bed, a religious act is spirituality in action—a necessary expression of a relationship with God.

A person can't be truly wise unless he engages his spirituality and confronts and expresses life's bigger questions, including the question of God. Where do I come from? Where am I going? Is there an afterlife? Is there eternal justice? Has God revealed himself to the world? Not all wise people will come up with the same answers to these questions, but they will all ask them, if they choose to have such courage.

Judy Clark is a wise person. Her path to spirituality and religion opened up when she reconnected with her Jewish roots. Her faith now gives her a spiritual matrix, a worldview through which to understand her own life and the lives of others. It has given her rituals, prayers, traditions, and connection to God. It was her growth in natural wisdom (a gift from God that she cultivated) that brought her to God, and it is her relationship with God that now nourishes her and increases her wisdom to discern what specifically God is asking of her in her unique life situation.

As John Paul II reflected in his book *Crossing the Threshold of Hope,* the question of God's existence touches the very heart of man's search for meaning and for wisdom.

> *One clearly sees that the response to the question "An Deus sit" (whether God exists) is not only an issue that touches the intellect; it is, at the same time, an issue that has a strong impact on all of human existence. It depends on a multitude of situations in which man searches for the significance and the meaning of his own existence. Questioning God's existence is intimately united with the purpose of human existence.*[1]

As human beings, when we are at our best we naturally look for what is good and true. We look for transcendence and meaning. We look for wisdom. We feel pulled to go beyond ourselves, to tend upward, toward the absolute. Saint Augustine expresses this truth on the very first page of his *Confessions* when he says: "You have made us for yourself, Oh Lord, and our hearts are restless until they rest in you."[2] At one time or another we all experience this restlessness. We long for something beyond the humdrum realities of the daily rat race. We want to know if everything ultimately makes sense or is merely the result of mindless chance and happenstance. We humans seem hard-wired to ask the bigger questions, including religious questions.

This is all to say that the closer we get to God the wiser we become. This is not to say that every great believer is wise in all things, nor that nonbelievers cannot be wise in many things, but belief in God radically changes—indeed, rectifies—our worldview. It makes the world around us intelligible at its deepest level. Rather than chance and randomness, order and intelligence emerge as the defining principles of the world. Belief in God can lead us to finding divine purpose behind things—the life-changing conviction that God "intends" things for us and is interested in our welfare. Do you see how integral is this type of living faith—the ability to discern what is the wise choice at hand, what God wants of you—to attaining the fullness of wisdom?

In the Judeo-Christian tradition, this discovery of God as the origin and purpose of all creation is wedded to love. God does not just "create" us or "know" us—he loves us. What is true for the grand scale is also true for each of our lives. Jesus declared that not even a sparrow falls from the sky without God knowing it, and he assured his followers that his care for us human beings is far greater. He said this to strengthen our trust in God and our belief in his providence in our lives.

Religious faith doesn't merely offer a framework to better understand the universe or our own lives. It isn't even just an intellectual pursuit that stops with conviction regarding God's existence. We can talk about God theoretically, but we can never begin to understand who he is or what he wants of us (discernment) until we let him into our lives. The "God question" should always end up as an existential question, meaning that it should touch every part of who we are. To the degree that we let God into our lives, he will come in as a welcomed guest and our friendship will grow. It's not dissimilar to human friendships, which grow when we spend time together and share both good times and bad. In our friendships, we take on a bit of our friends. We become like them. Personal contact and friendship with God brings us wisdom, since we are in relationship with wisdom itself.

I know that a willingness to fall in love with God and listen to his voice is a little scary. What will he say to us? What might he ask of us? This is where faith is experienced as both the problem and the solution. While it is a bit scary to listen to God's voice, if we have truly encountered God's love, we are even more consoled to know God will never ask of us anything that is not the very best for us.

So we find ourselves in need of courage once again. We need courage to engage our soul in the pursuit of God, to transform God-given spirituality into a religious response of love. We need courage not only to change the things we can but also to dare to confront life's larger questions, to seek wisdom in God himself and his purpose and plan for all of his creation.

God answers our three petitions—for serenity, courage, and wisdom—with one solution: the gradual transformation of our soul to think, feel, judge, and act more like him.

∞

Lord, I believe you are wisdom itself. You are truth, goodness, and beauty. You are the giver of life and the giver of purpose. Today, Lord, I will seek your face. I will invite you into my soul as a welcomed guest. Stay with me. Teach me. Comfort me. Lead me by the heart as I live out the life and mission you have blessed me with.

CHAPTER 33

The Whispers of God

❦

OVER THE CENTURIES, many of the holy men and women who have advocated setting some time aside for prayer have also suggested cultivating what they would call "the presence of God." This means learning to be aware of God's presence at all times, not just during prayer times. Awareness of his activity in the world opens our minds and hearts to the wisdom of seeing all things through his eyes. A wonderful homily dating all the way back to the sixth century AD offers this simple advice to disciples of Jesus:

> Indeed the soul should not only turn to God at times of explicit prayer. Whatever we are engaged in, whether it is care for the poor, or some other duty, or some act of generosity, we should remember God and long for God. The love of God will be as salt is to food, making our actions into a perfect dish to set before the Lord of all things.[1]

This brings us back again to the question of silence. Only when we pause in the midst of our activities can we hear the voice of God. And there's the rub: God does not shout to make himself heard; he whispers. In a celebrated passage from the biblical First Book of Kings, the prophet Elijah goes to the Mount of Horeb for a meeting with God. And under what aspect does God present himself? Here is the passage:

> *Now there was a great wind, so strong that it was splitting mountains and breaking rocks in pieces before the Lord, but the Lord was not in the wind; and after the wind an earthquake, but the Lord was not in the earthquake; and after the earthquake a fire, but the Lord was not in the fire; and after the fire a sound of sheer silence. When Elijah heard it, he wrapped his face in his mantle and went out and stood at the entrance of the cave. (1 Kings 19:11–13)*

God does not reveal himself in the fierce wind, nor in the earthquake, nor in the fire, but in silence. Our God is not a God of trumpets and gongs, but a God of whispers. We know this from experience from the way he speaks in our conscience, gently prodding, never imposing. And why is this? Why isn't God more forceful in making his presence known? Wouldn't more people believe in him? Wouldn't more people obey his will if he were to speak with greater power?

There is a young homeless man who spends his day on Forty-Ninth Street in Manhattan, just down the street from my office. Andrew has a little stand made of milk crates where he sells prints of New York City landmarks. Most people try to avoid him because he seems to be dealing with psychological issues of some sort. He is always talking to himself, and out loud. The things he says can be rather disturbing. He repeats over and over again that "people today are like zombies who only care about numbers and terrorists." That's the gist of it at least. Andrew makes a sale only when someone sees one of the prints from afar without hearing him talking to himself. Once the person gets close to the prints, Andrew's old social skills kick in and he is able to make the deal.

This young salesman has become a great blessing to me. Andrew may be sick and homeless, but on one unforgettable day in July he was the clear and undeniable voice of God for me.

I think I had met Andrew six months before. I usually saluted him as I walked by, and now and again I would offer to buy him lunch on the way back from mine. I am ashamed to say that I never bothered to ask his name. I didn't ask him because I didn't think it would make a difference. I didn't think he would care. I was pretty sure he only cared about talking to me about numbers, terrorists, and zombies.

But on this hot July day I was in a rush and I tried to avoid Andrew's stand altogether. As I began to cross the street I heard a loud voice calling, "Jonathan!" I turned around, expecting to encounter one of my coworkers, but instead I saw good ol' Andrew looking at me with a big smile. I was so shocked that he knew my name, and would use it, that I hurried toward him. I'm pretty sure he was smiling because he knew I was surprised that he knew my name, and I feared it was also because he had caught me avoiding him. "How do you know my name?" I asked him. "I've always known it," he said.

To this day I don't know if I had told him my name when we first met months before or if he asked someone for it. Either way, on that day God whispered to me in the voice and face of Andrew. This man who struggled so terribly with mental illness cared enough about me to learn my name. He called out to me when I was avoiding him. I hadn't known it, but he truly cared about our conversations, even though to me they had always been the same, always more or less useless.

God's whispers come in so many forms. After Andrew touched me so deeply that day, I can't help but treat him and others like him with reverence and holy deference. After all, God may be whispering to me in their voices, telling me how I need to change, how I need to love better and love more people. When we hear God's voice, no matter how quiet or unexpected it may be, we grow in wisdom.

I would hazard a guess that God chooses to manifest himself in whispers for at least four reasons. The first is God's total respect for human freedom. Our choices must be truly ours. We are, it would seem, the only creatures on earth that God created free. Birds don't spontaneously decide one year that they will no longer migrate to Florida but go to Mexico instead, or stay in upstate New York and brave out the winter there. They go where their instincts direct them. In this sense, animals never act below their nature, but neither do they ever act above their nature. They follow it perfectly. Human beings are different. Only humans can act like brute beasts or like angels. We can rise above mere nature, or we can sink below it. We are capable not only of acts of heroic generosity but acts of the most shameful pettiness. And it would seem that God wants us this way—free to accept or reject him, free to obey or disobey, free to give ourselves in love or to cling to ourselves in egotism.

God was willing to risk the possibility of millions of years of human disobedience and rebellion against him and against each other because, in his estimation, the times when we use that same freedom for the good—human love—are so good, so true, and so beautiful! Have you ever thought of it this way?

Another aspect of God's choice to respect our freedom by whispering to us is the fact that when he does speak out loud his voice is necessarily heard and obeyed. When he exclaims, "Let there be light," there is light, no questions asked. His word is imperative, and what he declares is done. When Jesus says to the turbulent Sea of Galilee, "Be still!" the sea obeys immediately. With us mortals, it is different. He does not compel us by his authority. He whispers, he suggests, he inspires. He gently prods but never twists our arm or obliges us to submit. He wants us to come to him freely and to obey him by choice, not by force. His respect for us is too great. This is wonderful, but also a little scary, since it makes our choices—and their consequences—ultimately our own.

A second reason God chooses not to shout but to whisper is his righteous jealousy. We find in the Book of Exodus that Moses commands: "You shall worship no other god, because the Lord is a jealous God" (Exodus 34:14). We typically think of jealousy as a fault. A jealous wife, for instance, may be hypersensitive to her husband's dealings with other women and suppose that things are going on even when they are not. God's jealousy, however, stems from his consuming love for us. He wants us for himself because he made us for himself. He does not want to share our loyalties with idols. A divided heart is an unhappy heart. And so he will not lower himself to compete in a shouting match with all the voices that vie for our attention. If we love money and celebrity and glory and pleasure, then he will not compete. He will not share the field with these contenders for our hearts. If we care more for what people think of us than what God thinks of us, he will wait patiently, but he will not impose himself or try to convince us otherwise. So he waits, like a patient lover, ready to take us back when we have realized that he alone satisfies our hearts.

Third, God whispers so that others cannot hear. God respects the privacy and interiority of our conscience and never makes that sacred inner sanctuary accessible to others—unless we ourselves choose to share it with others. Our conscience is meant to judge our own actions and intentions, not those of others. So no one else is privy to God's secret urgings to our hearts. He never makes them public. We can hear them and choose to follow them or not, without anyone else being aware. Only God knows. He offers us an intimacy that no one else can violate.

A fourth reason for God's whispering may be to save us from despair. If all of God's inspirations and instructions and corrections were put in our face at full volume all the time, we would recognize how far we fall short of his totally fair and reasonable expectations and we could be tempted to despair: "Leave me, Lord, for I am a sinful man." Instead, his urgings are accessible in that quiet voice for us to discover in silence, in prayer, one or two at a time, as our human frailty can handle them.

Christ said: "He who has ears to hear, let him hear." The choice to hear or not is ultimately our own. He offers us his own wisdom, but only if we are willing to close the door and listen to him in the silence of our hearts.

This can all be summed up by saying that God chooses to speak to you and to me in whispers because he is always so close to us that whispers are all he needs.

∞

Oh, Jesus, I believe you are next to me and speaking to me all the time. When my eyes and ears are open, I see you and hear your voice in your creation, in the Bible, in your Church, and in every circumstance of my life that you permit. Lord, today I recommit myself to listening to your whispers and doing what you command.

CHAPTER 34

The Root of All Wisdom

☙

IF SOMEONE asked you where wisdom comes from, what would you say? Maybe wisdom comes from reading good books, or from spending time with people of great knowledge. Maybe it comes from having lived a long life with many and varied experiences. Yet when the Bible speaks about wisdom, it doesn't say that it originates in careful consideration, or philosophical ponderings, or even many years of life experience. The root of wisdom, we read, is "fear of the Lord" (Proverbs 9:10). This may seem a little strange to us. Does God really want us to fear him? How does "fear" make us wise?

The Italian political philosopher Niccolò Machiavelli famously asks in his classic work *The Prince* whether a monarch should endeavor to be feared or to be loved. He answers this query, in his typical style, by saying: "It may be answered that one should wish to be both, but, because it is difficult to unite them in one person, is much safer to be feared than loved, when, of the two, either must be dispensed with."[1] In other words, being feared and being loved are both good, but since it is hard to be both, it is more expedient to be feared if a monarch must choose between the two. Machiavelli explains: "Men have less scruple in offending one who is beloved than one who is feared, for love is preserved by the link of obligation which, owing to the baseness of men, is broken at every opportunity for their advantage; but fear preserves you by a dread of punishment which never fails." At least for Machiavelli, fear seems to trump love when it comes to keeping one's subjects in line.

I can't imagine, however, that this was what the biblical author was thinking when he spoke of "fear of the Lord" as the beginning of wisdom. There is no doubt that God would rather be loved than feared. In a way, love and fear are even incompatible. Saint John himself wrote: "There is no fear in love, but perfect love casts out fear; for fear has to do with punishment, and whoever fears has not reached perfection in love" (1 John 4:18). So why do we Christians still speak of "fear of the Lord" as if it were a good thing?

"Fear of the Lord" is one of the seven gifts of the Holy Spirit. It has little to do with fear in the sense of the distressing emotion aroused by impending danger. In fact, Saint Augustine notes that fear is of several kinds, and that the fear of the Lord is not "human fear," but that fear of which it was said, "Fear Him that can destroy both soul and body into hell" (Matthew 10:28).[2] Quite simply, fear in this sense means "to heed," "to take seriously," or even "to honor as worthy of respect." To say we fear neither God nor man means that we care little for anyone else's opinion, even God's. To say that someone is a "God-fearing" person means that he or she cares more about what God thinks than about what others think and seeks to please him rather than people.

By now you know that Saint Catherine of Siena is one of my favorite doctors of the Church. She made an important distinction with respect to wisdom and fear of God. In her *Dialogue*, she frequently makes the distinction between what she calls "slavish fear" and "holy fear." One is the fear of servants or slaves, and the other that of sons and daughters. One breeds sadness and anxiety, the other joy and peace. And after posing a question similar to Machiavelli's, Catherine hears God give her the opposite answer. Servile fear is not enough for eternal life; love is essential. The old law was the law of fear; the new law is the law of love. When Jesus said to his followers, "I no longer call you servants, but friends," he was describing the difference between the old law and the new law.

Have you noticed that there is nothing more refreshing than being with someone who doesn't care what others think? These people are happier, more joyful and free, and they have no hidden agendas. In fact, they have no strictly personal agendas at all. What you see is what you get, and what you see is selflessness. On the other hand, it is usually obvious that someone who is trying, for selfish purposes, to impress people, get their vote, or otherwise win their approval is being fake. They are stifled and restricted, and they are not free. In that state of mind, no one can be fully happy.

I have been especially pleased by Pope Francis's continuous warning to the clergy about "clericalism." He has said that such career building is antithetical to our call to service. How true that is! The happiest young priests I know, for example, are the ones who genuinely don't want to be monsignors and bishops and who avoid doing anything with the intention of climbing the ecclesiastical ladder. How freeing it is to have no agenda other than love and to fear nothing other than displeasing God! If I'm doing what I should and still my boss or bishop doesn't like me, I will be fine. If I get the worst assignment possible, still, I will be just fine! Not only am I not climbing a ladder, but I don't even see one. I trust that Jesus himself will be my ladder on the day God calls me home to him. If this is true for clerics, it's just as true for laypeople. Who are you trying to please, and why? What are you living for? The wisdom that God wants for us will bring us ultimately to a place of great peace and joy.

It is healthy to ask ourselves why we do what we know we shouldn't do, and why we don't do what we ought to do. When our sin and selfishness are just signs of our weakness, we can do the best we can, ask trusted people for advice on how to overcome our deficiencies, and get back up after every fall. But sometimes there is a more fundamental problem: We haven't made a deep commitment to God. We are still living for ourselves. We do not have a "holy fear" of the Lord.

The fear of the Lord is the beginning of wisdom. If we look to God as our point of reference, if we turn to him as the one who defines what is important and what is not, and if we want to please him more than anything else, we have already embarked on the path of true wisdom. We have discovered the true measure of what is and what is not. If we fear the Lord rather than men, if we heed his word more than the cleverness of the world, we have already planted our trust where it belongs. That is indeed wisdom.

∞

Heavenly Father, although I have said it before, today I say it with deeper conviction: I choose to live for you! Increase in me holy fear of you, and you alone. Purify my intentions that I might only want to please you and to love others as you love them.

CHAPTER 35

Discernment

❧

THE POP SONG "Turn! Turn! Turn!" became an international hit in late 1965 when it was covered by the American folk-rock band The Byrds. Written by Pete Seeger in 1959, the song has the distinction of having the oldest lyrics of any number-one *Billboard* hit, since it was adapted entirely from the biblical Book of Ecclesiastes. These lyrics—often attributed to King Solomon—list a range of human activities that correspond to particular times, or seasons:

> *To everything there is a season, and a time to every*
> *purpose under the heaven:*
> *A time to be born, and a time to die; a time to plant,*
> *a time to reap that which is planted;*
> *A time to kill, and a time to heal; a time to break*
> *down, and a time to build up;*
> *A time to weep, and a time to laugh; a time to*
> *mourn, and a time to dance;*

A time to cast away stones, and a time to gather
stones together; a time to embrace, and a time
to refrain from embracing;
A time to get, and a time to lose; a time to keep,
and a time to cast away;
A time to rend, and a time to sow; a time to keep
silence, and a time to speak;
A time to love, and a time to hate; a time of war,
and a time of peace.

According to the lyricist, there is a proper time for everything—and by extension we could say that there is an improper time for everything as well. There is a time for dancing, to be sure, but that probably wouldn't be during a final exam or a friend's funeral. The virtue of discernment, or discretion, teaches us the proper time and place for everything and allows us to distinguish between things that seem almost the same. To discern means to separate. Discernment is wisdom in action, and a virtue attributed to God's word.

The word of God, we read in the Letter to the Hebrews, "is living and active, sharper than any two-edged sword, piercing until it divides soul from spirit, joints from marrow; it is able to judge the thoughts and intentions of the heart" (Hebrews 4:12). Here the word "judge" (*discretor* in Latin) means "to discern." A well-spoken word can rouse the weary, embolden the fainthearted, or soothe the troubled. But an ill-spoken word can have the opposite effect. It can embarrass, divide, perturb, and scandalize. And who can judge? Who can know the best time to act, or the best words to speak? This, too, is wisdom, a wisdom we humbly request from the Spirit of wisdom, God himself.

Holy Spirit,
inspire me to know what to think,
what I should say,
what I should silence,
what I should write,
what I should do,
how I should work for the good of all people,
the fulfillment of my mission
and the triumph of Christ's kingdom.

In his little book *The Spiritual Exercises,* Ignatius of Loyola, the founder of the Jesuits, taught that an important aspect of discernment on major issues is "discernment of spirits." "Spirits" here refers to the perceptible action of God in our souls leading us in a certain direction as we consider taking one path or another. We discover this divine action—the movement of the Spirit in our souls—over an extended period of time. Let me explain.

Not long ago I was in Rome with Cardinal Timothy Dolan and had the joy of cohosting his radio show on the Catholic Channel on SiriusXM radio. We had a live audience of college students and invited them to ask questions of the cardinal. One young man told the cardinal his emotional story of having broken up with his girlfriend the week before. He asked, "So, Cardinal Dolan, how do I know if I did the right thing?" The audience didn't know whether to laugh or cry. On the one hand, it was funny to hear the student ask Cardinal Dolan his advice about dating, and specifically about a girl whom the cardinal had never met. On the other hand, the question was so personal and fresh that everyone was sad for this young man. Either way, all were eager to hear the cardinal's response.

Now, Cardinal Dolan usually begins his answer to almost anything with a joke. It puts everyone at ease and opens the heart to the very serious answer he is about to give. But this time the cardinal got very serious. I think he recognized the question as a tough one, and an important one. He began by reminding this young man that when we are discerning God's will about an issue like this, there are usually certain things we can be sure of. For example, if his former girlfriend is married to someone else . . . she's not the right one. If he is already married to someone else . . . she's not the right one. If she doesn't share any of his values . . . she's probably not the right one. If he doesn't like her, or if she doesn't like him . . . she's definitely not the right one. If the people he trusts most all tell him that she is bad for him . . . she's probably not the right one.

When those basic questions are cleared up, the cardinal continued, and we still don't know what to do, it's usually the case that we need more discernment. In comes Ignatius's "discernment of spirits." Cardinal Dolan explained to this young man that discernment of spirits involves analyzing the state of our mind and heart over an extended period of time. Is there a lasting peace and serenity that come from following one or the other choices at hand? Over an extended period of time, are we better able to pray, commune with God, and love those around us when we are on this path rather than another?

As Cardinal Dolan reminded this young man, the discernment of spirits, the detection of divine action in our souls, kindly moving us in the direction that will be best for us, helps us to make wise choices. The wisdom to know the difference is as true as it is subtle. God is on our side. He is not waiting to punish us if we seek his will but get it wrong. All he asks of us is a heart and mind ready to listen and obey his whispers. God is truly the origin of all human wisdom, and for this we pray.

∞

Deep down I only want to do your will, O Lord. Sometimes my mind, heart, or body tells me that another way is better. Grant me today the gift of generosity as I discern your will. Gift me with your wisdom to discern the path I should take, in matters both large and small.

CHAPTER 36

Don't Avoid Risks—Take the Right Ones

❦

THE "wisdom to know the difference" speaks to us of a discerning spirit, a spirit not of timidity or of rashness, but one of clarity and purpose. We generally associate prudence with risk-aversion, the ability to control one's impulses and take the more careful and "prudent" path. For example, which of the following cases would you normally associate with the virtue of prudence?

1. A woman is offered a promotion to international vice president of her firm, and after weighing the options and discussing it with her husband, she accepts the job despite the toll it will take on her family life due to her increased travel and responsibilities.

2. A man is offered a partnership in a new business venture that promises probable profits in excess of 25 percent, but decides not to risk his family's capital and so declines the offer.

3. A woman is asked for her opinion on homosexual marriage and responds diplomatically to avoid offending sensibilities and endangering her job.

4. A man is invited on a business trip to Las Vegas, but knowing his weakness for alcohol and women and the values of
his coworkers, he opts out of the trip.

All of these are examples of people exercising what could
properly be described as prudence, but we are naturally
inclined to view the more cautious choices as the more prudent.
As we saw throughout the life of Jesus, however, prudence is
not only a matter of knowing what not to say or what not to do,
but also of knowing what to say and do even when feathers will
be ruffled, especially our own.

We can find a perfect illustration of this in the Gospel. Simon
Peter and the other apostles are rowing across the Sea of Galilee
in a violent storm (Matthew 14:22–33). They see Jesus walking
toward them across the water, and Peter shouts out, "Lord, if
it is really you, tell me to walk to you across the water." Mean-
while, the other apostles sit in the boat to watch what will
happen. Who is more prudent, Peter or the other apostles? We
would immediately think that the other apostles are much more
prudent, since they avoid the rash course of getting out of their
boat to try to walk across water in a storm. Yet when Peter says
this to Jesus, Jesus responds, "Come!" And Peter gets out of the
boat and begins walking toward him. Peter's total trust in the
Lord is a good and, ultimately, prudent exercise.

Thomas Aquinas describes prudence as the queen of virtues
and the "charioteer," with all the reins in her hand, who coor-
dinates all the other virtues as though they are horses pulling
the chariot. Drawing on this, the Catechism of the Catholic
Church promoted by John Paul II speaks of prudence as "the
virtue that disposes practical reason to discern our true good in
every circumstance and to choose the right means of achieving
it. . . . Prudence is 'right reason in action.' "[1]

As rationalistic as secular society can seem to be, I believe that reason has actually fallen from favor. There is more talk now about emotional decision-making, gut feelings, and sensitivity than about rational choices, which sound somehow cold and unfeeling. But in the end, good action responds to good reason. For a Christian, this is reason enlightened by faith.

Let's take a simple analogy from the world of sports. Think of a baseball player at bat. He has choices to make, but they are basically reduced to two: to swing or not to swing at a given pitch. Yet despite the simplicity of the decision, there are numerous factors he must weigh, often in an instant. Here the richness of prudent decision-making becomes more evident. There is, on the one hand, the possibility of lost opportunities (the danger of waiting too long, or of missing the best pitch). In other words, there are consequences if the batter fails to act. Prudence does not always counsel inaction but knows that both action and inaction have their advantages and their risks. The batter must avoid the dual dangers of perfectionism (waiting for the perfect pitch) and negligence (assuming any pitch would be fine, they're all the same).

Second, the batter must assess the offer before him: the quality of the pitch. Is the pitch a strike or a ball? Is it high or low? Within the batter's range or outside it?

Third, prudence also demands self-knowledge. The batter must bear in mind his own objective strengths, weaknesses, and inclinations or tendencies: what pitches does he prefer (or is a sucker for)? How well does he hit low pitches, high pitches, curves, or sliders? In all our decisions, we need to consider not only the choice to be made but the one making it!

Fourth, our batter must take into consideration a number of circumstances that will affect the way he approaches his decision. What is the count? Can he afford to be wrong on the next pitch? How many men are on base? What is the score of the game? What inning is it? If the count is 3-0, the batter can relax more than he can if the count is 0-2. If his team is whipping the opponent, he can be more at ease than when the score is close.

I told you earlier about my gut-wrenching choice to leave the religious order of missionary priests that I was a member of for fifteen years and move to New York to be a parish priest. I had serious concerns as I was leaving my religious family that my choice was imprudent, that perhaps the best thing to do would have been to continue the course. But there was something inside of me—I now know it to be the movement of the Spirit—that nudged me hard and long enough that I chose to push out into deep uncharted waters. In this case, I can't say I initially followed the recommended path of "discernment of spirits." That came later. In the moment, I just knew that God was leading me to move forward, and quickly. Looking back on what would occur within the religious order over the next few years, I see why God spurred me to act so quickly. If I had waited any longer I would have felt obliged to stay and be part of the impending reform process ordered by the Vatican. That was surely what God asked of others, but for some reason he didn't ask that of me.

I bring this personal story back into our journey of seeking God's peace through serenity, courage, and wisdom to demonstrate that in the end these are all gifts of God that come in personalized packages. It was God who showed me the wise and prudent thing to do in that moment. My decision wasn't the outcome of making a rational study of the situation or applying a generic formula.

Finally, habits are important. As a virtue, prudence is not a good action but a good habit. A batter cannot possibly analyze everything in the moment. He needs to rely on his instincts. His instincts are not innate tendencies, however, but learned patterns of behavior that have been imprinted by repetition. We should never confuse experience (making good, rational decisions) with simple intuition (having a gut feeling). The repetition of deliberate, intelligent, good actions creates a good habit, so that eventually such good actions become second nature. At bat, it doesn't matter how many books you have read on baseball. It matters how you have conditioned yourself to do the right thing in a split second, when there is no time to calculate all the dimensions of the decision at hand. So it is in the spiritual life. The best decision-maker will be the one who has formed the habit of listening to the voice of God and following it wherever it leads.

The "wisdom to know the difference" is the fruit of the Spirit, and it usually looks like the virtue of prudence. We ask for it, but we also work on it. A good habit plus the grace of the Holy Spirit is the perfect combination to act as we should— with serenity, courage, and wisdom.

∞

Heavenly Father, you took the ultimate risk of giving humanity free will. You have bet on me to say yes to your love and forgiveness. Give me that same spirit of prudent risk-taking, against the base inclinations of the flesh that lead me down and in favor of your perfect plan for my life.

CHAPTER 37

A Life of Purpose and Meaning

❧

ARE YOU getting wiser as you read? Even if you don't feel it, my bet is that you are. That's the way God seems to impart wisdom. He feeds us truth in bite sizes, and even as we are processing it some of it sticks to our spiritual bones and becomes part of who we are. Without realizing it, we begin to think and judge differently. We start to give greater value to important things. We become more patient and trusting in God's power and will to intervene when we can't. We become less concerned about what others think of us and more attentive to how God sees us.

Becoming the wise men and women God wants us to be doesn't happen in the same way, or in the same order, for everyone. Just as there are a gazillion ways to put together a jigsaw puzzle, we each blaze our own path to the embrace of the wisdom of God. Each of these chapters is intended to be a piece of the puzzle. Take your time to look at each piece. Imagine where you might place it, then use it or set it aside for later. You may want to come back at some point in the future and reexamine the chapter in relation to where you are then, reconsidering what's missing, what's good, and what needs to be removed or shifted in order to fit together your mosaic of truth.

We spend much of our lives worrying about how to get things done. Much of our training in school is directed at learning how to do things. We make ourselves useful and "hirable" by acquiring competency in different areas. Our value to others increases as we pick up know-how and expand our repertoire of capabilities, our "skill set." Moreover, as we do so we also gain self-esteem and a healthy sense of independence. We learn to use a computer, to drive, to cook, to do accounting, to conduct experiments, to communicate, to solve problems, and so on. These capabilities make us feel like we have a good handle on life, and they are tremendously important—as long as we're aware of a still more important dimension to our existence: the meaning behind all our capabilities. If wisdom is the ability to discern what is important, then we need to know the relative importance of our skills and capabilities in our lives, both for now and for eternity.

Unlike any other creature, we humans can determine the motives for our actions, and these motives make us who we are. *Why do I get up in the morning? Why do I take care of a sick member of my family? Why do I treat people in a certain way? Why do I go to school or work? Why do I stay in a relationship?* These questions are ultimately more important than the mere mechanics of how each of these actions is carried out. Taking time to consider the "whys" behind our actions is hugely important in the pursuit of wisdom.

That great master of meaning Viktor Frankl, reflecting on his experience in the Nazi concentration camps, came to this conclusion:

A human being is not one thing among others; things deter-mine each other, but man is ultimately self-determining. What he becomes—within the limits of endowment and envi-ronment—he has made out of himself. In the concentration camps, for example, in this living laboratory and on this test-ing ground, we watched and witnessed some of our comrades behave like swine while others behaved like saints. Man has both potentialities within himself; which one is actualized depends on decisions but not on conditions.[1]

Frankl's profound belief in the freedom of the human person was based on his experience of how different people responded to identical circumstances in radically different ways. Some allowed themselves to be molded by their environment, while others decided for themselves what sort of people they were going to be. And as he poignantly put it, in the horrific condi-tions of the concentration camp, he saw "some of our comrades behave like swine while others behaved like saints." Through-out his amazing little book *Man's Search for Meaning*, Frankl returns over and over to a key point. "There is nothing in the world," Frankl insists, "that would so effectively help one to survive even the worst conditions as the knowledge that there is meaning in one's life. There is much wisdom in the words of Nietzsche: 'He who has a why to live for can bear almost any how.' "[2] It is meaning that motivates our actions and liberates us from the angst of an absurd existence.

Some meaning comes from our willing it. We create it by imprinting a sense, value, and motivation on our choices and actions. We choose to do certain things in a certain way for a certain reason. We create a life for ourselves by our decisions, and every single moment fits into the bigger picture of the story, the "living autobiography," that each of us is writing. But along with the meaning we create ourselves is another meaning written into human existence that is not of our own making, but is there to be discovered. Things fit into a still larger picture that is human history itself, a complex web of relationships, events, and actions.

Some people disagree with this idea, of course. They would argue that the universe has no meaning in itself, but only that which we give it. One must fully accept the truth, they would contend, even if that means accepting a universe with no meaning whatsoever. After all, it is better to embrace absurdity than to live in willful self-deceit. I would agree with this wholeheartedly. A lie with good intentions or happy consequences is still a lie. I am also firmly convinced, however, that human life, and every tiny moment of it, is infused with meaning. It is there to be unearthed. The universe is intelligible, as both atheists and believers agree. Otherwise, the natural sciences could not function. There must be laws and patterns in nature in order for the natural sciences to have any claim to universality and predictability. Where does this meaning come from? Is it the result of chance or the product of a creating intelligence?

You know what I think because I've given my life to the answer. God is the creating intelligence behind you and me and all creation. And the existential meaning and purpose of things can be found in him alone. Let me tell you how I experience this in day-to-day life.

A long time ago I decided that if God made me and has a plan for me, and if that plan is first and foremost about getting to heaven and bringing with me as many people as I can, as the Bible tells me, then I should approach my decisions about everything in this life with a simple question: does this created thing or person or organization or activity help me to reach this goal, or is it a distraction? To be honest, I often fail to even ask myself the question, and even when I do, sometimes I prefer the distraction to the truth. But this fundamental option that I have made (Ignatius of Loyola calls it the "principle and foundation") is a life-changer. This simple question and its answer give spiritual meaning to what I am doing.

If you have a spouse and a family and you have to decide whether to move to another city on account of a job offer, daring to ask yourself this question, I promise you, will make the right choice much clearer. And then when you make your choice, and it's a tough one that makes your children complain and your spouse have second thoughts, well, these consequences may not be fun, but you have good reason to keep going! Behind your action is spiritual purpose that will bring you and your family closer to God.

We can take comfort in knowing that our effort to make the wise choice through discernment of God's will is one that will always be blessed, even if the short-term outcome is disappointing. A few years ago a family approached me and asked me if the parish church could help them financially, as they were going through a terrible crisis of simultaneous unemployment and the sickness of their youngest child. The parish had a policy of not giving out money to individuals but rather supporting programs that provided services to the needy. I referred this family to various organizations, but it turned out that they were not able to offer enough support to solve their problem. The parents were both out of work, and the family of six was about to be evicted from their apartment, even as they were trying to attend to their youngest daughter, who was in a hospital in the neighborhood. Their situation was desperate, and I couldn't walk away from it. I decided to ask two of my friends to go in with me on the payment of six months of the family's rent, to give them time to get back on their feet without having to move away from the hospital. We each chipped in $2,000. When I received the checks, I went with the father of the family to the bank and opened up an account in his name. It was his first bank account. Two weeks later, the family moved out of the apartment, without having paid rent, and I haven't heard from them since.

That was a hard pill to swallow. Of course I felt betrayed by this family, but also embarrassed in front of my generous friends. Was my choice wise? Not really. Will it be blessed by God? Absolutely. The short-term outcome of our choices is much less important than the sincere pursuit of God's will. Because we believe in heaven, righteous choices are always the best choices, even when we get them wrong.

The ordinary path to wisdom leads us to ask the tough questions regarding the meaning in the world and in our lives, and then to act in harmony with the truth we discover.

∾

Father, there is so much on my plate, so much to do, and so many distractions that I often find myself just floating down the stream of life. I don't want to do this because I know I am missing out on your plan for me to be united with you in heart and in action. Grant me the wisdom today to do everything with loving purpose.

CHAPTER 38

Christian Wisdom?

&

T HE GREAT Christian apologist C. S. Lewis once wrote a delightfully provocative essay on the idea of Christian literature, culled from a paper he delivered to a religious society at Oxford.[1] He asks whether there is any such thing as "Christian literature," and if so, how it might differ from secular literature. His main argument is that the rules for good literature are the same for Christians and non-Christians alike. He writes, "I question whether it has any literary qualities peculiar to itself. The rules for writing a good passion play or a good devotional lyric are simply the rules for writing tragedy or lyric in general." He goes on to use a jocose example: asking whether there is any such thing as a Christian cookbook, he rightly concludes: "Boiling an egg is the same process whether you are a Christian or a Pagan." Lewis is right, of course. It would be patently absurd to speak of Christian mathematics or a Christian periodic table of the elements, as if somehow Christians followed a different set of rules when engaged in algebra or chemistry.

Truth is truth after all, so truth for a Christian should coincide with truth for a non-Christian. That seems to be common sense. So why would we speak about Christian wisdom as if it's somehow different from the common wisdom of mankind? It is no doubt true that everything that is really good for humanity is equally good for the Christian, and vice versa. Christianity elevates man but doesn't change his nature.

Christian wisdom, if there is such a thing—and I think there is—cannot be wisdom that is valid for Christians but not for everyone else. It must be something else. It is not an esoteric, gnostic sort of teaching reserved for a few enlightened initiates. It must consist, rather, in that superior wisdom that Christ came to reveal to all of humanity. Christians believe that God himself became man to reveal to us the truth about human existence. Jesus Christ is God, but he is also man. If in him we know God, we also know man—the ideal man—as he (or she) was meant to be. If we want to know what it means to be truly human and what is most important in life, we find answers to these questions in Christ's life. Christian wisdom, then, embraces the sometimes counterintuitive truths about human life that correspond to God's way of seeing things—which, after all, is the absolutely objective and pure way of seeing them as they are.

Christian wisdom surpasses merely human wisdom, without ever contradicting it. It surpasses human wisdom because it comes from God himself. Christianity offers basic guidelines for evaluating the different aspects of human existence and for assigning to them the weight they deserve. Having already seen that wisdom discerns between what is important and what is not, we are helped immensely in that discernment by the criteria offered by Christianity. Christianity teaches, for instance, that eternity is more important than temporality, that God's will is more important than merely pragmatic considerations, and that persons are more important than things.

The elements of Christian wisdom are worth pondering, so we will devote the next few chapters to exploring them.

CHAPTER 39

I've Got Heaven on My Mind

❦

IN 2009, Suzy Welch published her best-selling book *10-10-10: A Life-Transforming Idea*.[1] It's a guide to prudent decision-making based on a very simple premise. We often make bad choices because we act on the spur of the moment, according to what we feel like right now rather than according to reason. To escape from that trap, Welch recommends slowing down and asking ourselves how we will feel about this decision ten minutes from now, ten months from now, and ten years from now (10-10-10). Prudent decision-making requires getting out of the present moment in order to bring objectivity to our decisions and moving beyond passion and emotion in order to act with reason.

Welch is right. Many times we say things that we immediately regret but can't take back. If we could simply bite our tongue for a moment, long enough to think of how we will feel about those words ten minutes later, we'd save ourselves much embarrassment and many regrets. Ten minutes gives us time to cool down, especially when we're feeling the more vehement passions of anger and pride. Before we utter an unkind or hurtful word or shoot off a harsh email, a moment's consideration is in order.

This works for the mid- and long term as well. Asking ourselves how we will feel about a certain choice ten months or ten years from now, when all emotion is removed from the picture, can definitely help us make prudent decisions that we will always be happy with. Often our advice to others (as objective third parties) is spot-on, while our own choices don't shine with the same good sense. How will we evaluate a business decision, a divorce, a move, or a romantic fling ten months from now, or ten years from now? Engaging in this thought exercise to eliminate our present feelings can effectively bring our own good advice and real decision-making into sync.

As good as Welch's advice is, I cannot help but think that the most important reference point is missing. In the Christian tradition, we learn to evaluate our actions not only by the light of the future but especially by the light of eternity. To be truly wise, we must have a sense of what things are worth from God's perspective. In his truly life-changing *Spiritual Exercises,* Saint Ignatius of Loyola includes a meditation on death. This meditation has nothing to do with any gruesome medieval fixation with skulls and skeletons, but rather reflects the very wise principle that we should try to evaluate our present actions by considering what we will appreciate on our deathbed. It's spiritually healthy—Ignatius reasons—to live now the way we would like to be found at death, when we will look back on our lives from God's perspective. What will we value then? What will we regret? What will seem most precious and what will seem simply a lamentable waste of time and talents?

An eternal perspective puts a whole new spin on Welch's method. Instead of considering our present choices according to what we will value some minutes, months, or years from now, how about considering them according to what we will value when this short life is over? At that moment, what will you prefer: to have perfected your golf swing or to have learned humility and patience? What will seem more important: to have made millions of dollars or to have loved God and served your brothers and sisters? What will you value more: Sunday Mass or the extra hours of sleep?

The great medieval mystic Thomas à Kempis offers similar advice to Ignatius's, drawing on Jesus's teaching. In his spiritual classic *The Imitation of Christ*, he gives his readers the following sage counsel:

> *In every deed and every thought, act as though you were to die this very day. If you had a good conscience you would not fear death very much. It is better to avoid sin than to fear death. If you are not prepared today, how will you be prepared tomorrow? Tomorrow is an uncertain day; how do you know you will have a tomorrow?*[2]

Jesus asks the most important question of all for determining the true value of things: "What does it profit a man if he gains the whole world but loses his soul?" (Matthew 16:26). If our 10-10-10 works only for this life but not for eternity, we are still missing what is most important. No matter how good and prudent our choices seem, we need to measure them against our true, final horizon: eternity.

There is a wonderful polyphonic piece for Holy Saturday that I used to sing—poorly—back when I was in seminary. Written by Tomás Luís de Victoria, it is called "Judas Mercator Pessimus" (roughly translated as "Judas, the Worst Businessman"). It relates in very deep and sober tones that Judas was the worst possible merchant because he traded in what was most precious (Jesus!) for thirty pieces of silver. He was willing to hand over the author of life itself for a little momentary gain, just as Esau traded his birthright for a plate of pottage.

There was a time during my seminary studies when I was struggling tremendously with whether I should continue along the path toward priesthood and full-time service within the Church. The most intense period of doubt lasted for about six months, and I felt almost no positive spiritual sentiment during that time. I didn't want to pray. I didn't feel holy or spiritual or anything close to that. And I certainly felt no desire to become a priest. At the height of my negativity and doubt, I walked into a church in Bridgeport, Connecticut, where I had never been before. As it turned out, a priest was hearing confessions, and there was nobody in line. I went in to do my confession, and I told the priest what I was going through. The priest was so old that I don't know if he could even hear what I was saying. He didn't offer me any spiritual advice about the sins I confessed, but what he did say turned my life upside down. "Young man, keep in mind that the devil wants you to be a good man, and just a good man." Like a knife to the heart, I knew I was being tempted to mediocrity. I was depressed because I was fighting with the temptation to live my life my way rather than to live God's gift of life to me his way . . . with my eyes set on eternity.

Jesus often recommended to his disciples that they "be prepared"—not just like Boy Scouts ready for an unexpected night in the forest, but ready at a moment's notice to meet their Creator and render an accounting of their lives. He warns us that that day will appear "like a thief in the night" (1 Thessalonians 5:2) and reminds us that no one knows "the day or the hour" (Matthew 24:36).

This admonition to be prepared shouldn't turn us into joyless, boring fuddy-duddies but into true Christians. Every good thing has its place, but not all good things are equal in importance. When we look back on things from the perspective of eternity, I'm confident we will desire above all to see a beautiful life, a life well lived, a life forged by decisions made in the light of eternity! To cite Thomas à Kempis once again, "How happy and prudent is he who tries now in life to be what he wants to be found in death!"

Time and again in his parables Christ emphasizes the relative value of temporal goods compared to eternal goods. He encourages his followers to keep their sights fixed on heaven and not to get bogged down in the fleeting pleasures and riches that the world has to offer. In the clearest of terms, he contrasts the passing goods of temporal existence with the permanent goods of eternity:

> *Do not worry about your lives and what you are to eat or your bodies and how you are to clothe them, because life means more than food and the body more than clothing. Look at the ravens: they do not sow or reap, they have no barns, yet God feeds them. And how much more are you worth than the birds! . . . But you, you must not set your hearts on things to eat or things to drink; nor must you worry. It is the pagans of this world who set their hearts on all these things. Your Father well knows you need them. No; set your hearts on his Kingdom, and these other things will be given you as well. (Luke 12:22–31)*

Saint Paul, too, exhorts the members of the early Church to conserve this scale of values, to become "new men" with a new set of criteria and values. These values should distinguish the Christian from the nonbeliever. In one passage Paul says: "And so if you have risen with Christ, seek the things that are above, where Christ is seated at God's right hand. Aspire to heavenly things, not to the things of the earth" (Colossians 3:1–2).

When weighing up the true worth of things, Christian wisdom looks to what will last. Just as we would be silly to spend as much for a pair of shoes that will wear out in two weeks as for a pair that will last ten years, we would be foolish to pursue perishable goods with the same zeal as we pursue imperishable ones. Certain things last for the long haul. Others are destined to fall far short.

We have all heard the expression "You can't take it with you." All the stuff we have when we die will remain behind. Others will divide it up or throw it away. But there are some things we take with us—things that last for all eternity. When addressing himself to the Corinthians, Saint Paul writes: "We have no eyes for things that are visible, but only for things that are invisible; for visible things last only for a time, and the invisible things are eternal" (2 Corinthians 4:18). Paul ties visible things to this world and invisible things to what lasts forever. And he recommends that we place our hearts on the things that will last.

This doesn't mean that Christians are to neglect the things of this world. Material things are not bad. God made the world and all that is in it, so all of it is intrinsically good. It would be foolish—and rather boring—to despise the great things in life as somehow evil. It follows that we have a responsibility to take care of these good things. Our health, the environment, our wealth—responsible stewardship of all these things is part of what it means to be a good Christian. After all, Jesus says that on Judgment Day we will be examined on some very material things: whether we have fed the poor, clothed the naked, and visited the sick, and not just on whether we have prayed well.

But still, the hierarchy remains. Spiritual things are incorruptible, tied to eternity, whereas material things necessarily pass away. We value our looks, our bank accounts, and our vacations, but we must keep in mind that they are all slipping through our fingers at every moment and will not last forever. We will not, in Jesus's words, store up for ourselves a treasure on earth instead of where it really counts—in heaven (see Matthew 6:19–20). Youth and beauty are great examples of this. No matter how hard we work out at the gym and how much makeup we apply to our faces, our youth passes away and we cannot get it back. I'm frequently blown away when I see on the streets of Manhattan the extreme measures taken by some people to try to reverse the inevitable. Rather than desperately clinging to youth, wise people peacefully let it go and embrace every stage of life as the best one.

A Christian is called to look at the world differently than a nonbeliever does. For a nonbeliever, this life is all we have. For a Christian, we aren't home yet. We are pilgrims passing through a foreign land. Our true homeland lies beyond this life. Most Christians believe this, but rarely live it. How different life would be if we always had this in mind and lived accordingly!

Jesus was radical in his teaching. He kept upsetting the status quo and the way people saw things. This was especially true in his way of evaluating what is important and distinguishing it from what is unimportant. For example, when a poor widow contributes two copper coins to the temple treasury, Christ assures those around him that her gift has more worth than the prodigious donations of the rich. "Because these gave from their surplus, but she from the little she had, has put in everything she possessed, all she had to live on" (Mark 12:44). From a purely rational perspective, this is absurd. Two pennies can never be greater than large contributions. But Jesus tells us that in God's eyes it is.

On the other hand, Jesus upbraids the Pharisees for flipping the scale of values upside down. They wash the outsides of cups and dishes, he says, and neglect the more important matters of the law: "justice, mercy, good faith" (Luke 11:39–42). He tells us that what is going on in our hearts matters more than what is purely external. It is more important to practice the virtues of mercy and justice than to wash our hands correctly before eating.

As we have already seen, when asked which of the laws is the most important, Jesus does not hesitate to highlight love of God and love of neighbor as the sum and substance of the law, and far more important than any burnt offering. When the disciples get into an argument about who among them is the most important, Jesus stops them in their tracks by placing a little child in their midst and proclaiming that the child is the most important. What the world despises, God often finds to be of great worth.

All of this tells us that Christianity offers a new vision of human existence, a way of seeing and evaluating all the events and activities of human life. This vision is based on the truth about man, about his destiny, and about his relations with God and with the world.

Christian wisdom doesn't scorn God's creation or life on earth, but it does put them into perspective. That is where the wisdom to know the difference starts—with remembering eternity when making decisions.

∞

Lord, I know I am not home yet. You have given me this life as a taste of the life to come. But you know that I'm often distracted. I live as if the here and now is all that matters. Give me, Lord, wisdom to know the difference between those things I should fight for and those things I should let go, all in pursuit of the things that will last.

CHAPTER 40

God's Will or Mine?

❧

THERE ARE lots of good reasons as well as bad reasons for doing what we do. I remember a fascinating psychology course in college, called "Behavior in Organizations," in which we looked at what motivates people to make the choices they do. Money, fame, pleasure, philanthropy, and countless other incentives can motivate a person to act. Some motivations are rational, others are emotional, and most are a combination of things. A characteristically Christian wisdom places God's will above all of these. If we have made a fundamental commitment to living our earthly life as preparation for heaven, then in discerning what is truly important in life, nothing trumps doing what we think God wants us to do in order to get there—in other words, God's will.

This makes sense for a couple of reasons. First, since God made all that is, he knows his design better than anyone. He understands how things work, how they should fit together, and how human freedom should be used. We become wise when we plug into his wisdom, when we seek to integrate our decisions into his will.

But perhaps more importantly still, God's will marks out the road map for human happiness. A critical tenet of Christian faith is that God is love, and therefore everything he wills is an expression of that love. God wills only good things for us—the best things in fact. It is wise to follow the will of the one who seeks nothing but our good and knows where it is to be found. There is no doubt that this was the policy Jesus followed and taught. He said that doing the Father's will was his "food" (John 4:34), and that he always did what pleased "the one who sent me" (John 8:29). This policy carried over to his followers as well, since "whoever does the will of my Father in heaven is my brother and sister and mother" (Matthew 12:50).

It isn't always easy to know what God wants from us. Sure, we know a few things he doesn't want us to do (think of that well-known list of actions like theft, murder, and lying), but on the positive side it can get cloudier. Once in a while people in the Bible would receive visits from angels or get messages in dreams, but God doesn't seem to communicate this way with us very often. Mostly, we have to make the best decisions we can, through study, prayer, and consultation, and trust that God will bless us for our effort to know and do his will.

That doesn't mean, however, that we are walking in the dark. We do, after all, have a pretty good idea of what sort of people God wants us to be, and that is a really good start. A generous, forgiving, helpful, faithful, single-hearted person already knows how to act in just about every situation. If that isn't God's will, I don't know what is! And if God has special messages for us outside of the normal course of events, and if we are men and women with a consistent prayer life, he will surely find a way to let us know!

Most important is to have made the fundamental commitment to God: "Lord, I want to do your will." This profound choice to trust God is already very pleasing to him. A person who sincerely seeks God's will above all else has discovered some of the deepest wisdom there is.

I think one of the big surprises that await us in eternity is to see who life's great winners and losers are. Things we judge now by earthly standards will no doubt look different when we stand before God. I am always struck by Jesus's parable of the rich man and Lazarus. The rich man lives in a huge mansion, dresses in fine clothes, and feasts extravagantly. Lazarus is a poor beggar covered with sores who sits outside the gate of the rich man's house. The rich man is surely the talk of the town and invited to all the best parties. Everybody knows his name and wants to be his friend. And yet today we know him as simply "the rich man." Lazarus, on the other hand, is avoided by the people of his day. He is the consummate "loser" who has to make his living eating the scraps that people give him when he begs. And yet we know Lazarus now by name, and as Jesus told us, he was comforted in the bosom of Abraham.

What was the major difference between the two men? It's certainly not that one was rich and the other poor. It was, rather, that one lived for himself and sought the fulfillment of his own will, while the other sought the face of God even in his misery. One was foolish and the other wise.

On this path toward wisdom, sometimes all it takes is a change in our thought patterns. Instead of having our own will—what we want to do—as the axis of our thought and activity, we can decide to seek and do God's will. Over time this will alter our idea of success. Whereas before we may have become disheartened over small things, now we remember that the final victory is the one that counts. And this victory is not economic, social, or political. It is spiritual! No matter what happens to us, no matter what people do to us, no matter our state of health or wealth, our real success in life is not at risk. Our goal is to be with God!

Also making this point was another text I read in college, *The Consolation of Philosophy,* written by an ancient Christian philosopher named Boethius. One of Boethius's main proposals is that nothing that passes away can constitute our true good. What is temporary passes away, and what is eternal lasts forever. In God's eyes, what is "good news" and "bad news," really? Is there any good—besides God alone—that cannot be used for our detriment? Is there any "bad" that God cannot turn to good? How often I remember the consoling words of Saint Paul: "For those who love God, all things work together for good" (Romans 8:28).

There is a Taoist story that makes this point very well. An old farmer has worked his crops for many years. One day his horse runs away. Upon hearing the news, his neighbors come to visit.

"Such bad luck," they say sympathetically.

"We'll see," the farmer replies.

The next morning the horse returns, bringing with it three other wild horses.

"How wonderful," the neighbors exclaim.

"We'll see," replies the old man.

The following day the old man's son tries to ride one of the untamed horses, is thrown, and breaks his leg. The neighbors again come to offer their sympathy on the old man's misfortune.

"We'll see," he answers.

The day after, military officials come to the village to draft young men into the army. Seeing that the son's leg is broken, they pass him by. The neighbors congratulate the farmer on how well things have turned out.

"We'll see," says the farmer.

Every experience of our lives on earth, good or bad, is tinged with uncertainty and precariousness. Every joy is fragile, like a crystal figurine that could break at a moment's notice. The hour will come, however, when a final piece of good fortune will befall us, good fortune that no one will ever take away and no further misfortune can ever sully. It will be the day when we hear from the mouth of our Lord those blessed words: "Well done, good and faithful servant. Come and join in your master's happiness." At that point the fear that accompanies uncertainty will end forever. All contingency will be replaced by permanence. In the end, true wisdom consists in this. The world as we know it is passing away. Both pleasure and pain will fade into distant memory, with no lasting residue in our souls. It is the final victory that matters, and to know this and live accordingly is wisdom—Gospel truth.

∞

Lord, there are so many things that glitter and shine. Some are good for me, some are not. But deep in my heart I know you are the only one who can satisfy my deepest longings, the things that will make me flourish. Give me strength today to seek your will above everything else. I will do this out of love for you.

CHAPTER 41

Persons over Things

❧

A FINAL ASPECT of Christian wisdom is the primacy of persons over things. Jesus assures us that the Father has counted every hair on our head, so important is each one of us to him (Luke 12:7). And although God forgets not a single sparrow, we are worth more than many sparrows, Jesus tells us. Things are to be used; persons are to be loved. Every single person has infinite worth to God, so much so that the Good Shepherd will leave ninety-nine sheep and go search out the one that is lost (Luke 15:4).

In God's eyes, no one is just a "number." No one is expendable. No one slips through the cracks. He keeps his eye on each one of us and loves each of us in a unique and perfect way. I remember being told as a kid that even if I were the only person on earth, Jesus would have died on the cross for me. That thought really amazed me. Jesus didn't just die for "humanity"—he died for me! That must be what Saint Paul has figured out too when he says that "I live by faith in the Son of God, who loved me and gave himself for me" (Galatians 2:20). Paul puts that statement in the first person singular: "for *me*."

What an awesome thought that God loves each of us with that singularity.

There is nothing more powerful or life-changing than this conviction of God's radical love for each one of us as his child. It changes us from the inside out. For if God loves us so completely, we can't help but try to love him and others in a similar way. How can we look at other human beings with disdain if Christ loves them so much that he would have died just for them? How can we despise what Christ loves? In this way, it's easy to see that a Christian is called to be totally inclusive. We are to love everyone, with no exceptions.

Although Christ came for the sick, the sinful, the weak . . . for all of us . . . Christianity is not for the faint of heart. The great commandment of love can be the hardest thing in the world to live out. Once in a while love comes naturally, and then it is easy. But this is the exception. Most of the time love requires courage, self-sacrifice, and lots of patience. We really need a heart like Christ's to love people the way he wants us to. How beautiful but how gut-wrenching, for example, is the command to forgive those who trespass against us and to love even our enemies! When someone who has intentionally hurt us is not even repentant yet, it takes tremendous courage to respond with love, as Jesus did himself: "Forgive them, Father, for they know not what they do" (Luke 23:34). Imitating Jesus is always wise.

Practicing Christian wisdom means trying our best to live for others, always. It means always putting people first. This is a real challenge for me. I start off the day with a to-do list of all the tasks I need to take care of. I am "project-oriented" and unconsciously define a good day as one when I can check off a lot of things on my list. But people are not quantifiable tasks. We can never put a check mark after their names, as if they were a project. They are always there, not as things to deal with but rather as neighbors to love.

The parable of the Good Samaritan always calls me to task, especially when I am reading it out loud in front of my congregation. You probably remember that the first guy who passes by the man in need is a priest! He is busy, probably on his way to a meeting or to give a talk. He is an important fellow and can't be bothered. So he just walks on past the poor man who has been beaten up and robbed. The priest makes a bad choice. He doesn't put people first—he puts "things" first: his time, his schedule, his tasks. And Jesus tells us that he is not a neighbor to the man who has been beaten up. The priest is not wise.

Christian wisdom tells us that nothing is more important than another person. And it doesn't matter who the person is—a little child, a poor person, an illiterate or foul-smelling or unpleasant or arrogant person. It doesn't matter. That person is important to God and should be important to us.

The incarnation of Jesus as Word among us makes wisdom immensely practical for us Christians. Because we have come to see, hear, and almost touch Jesus in the Gospel, we don't need prophets, kings, or angels to tell us God's will. We don't need wise men to decipher for us the meaning of the constellations or to predict the future for us. So often we can simply ask ourselves: What would Jesus of Nazareth want us to do? Is this is a time when we should let go of our insistence on being treated fairly? What would Jesus do? Should we overlook something that bothers us about another person—a sister-in-law, a mother-in-law, a coworker—or should we confront them? We ask what Jesus would do. When we are unsure or confused, we have the lives of the heroic Christians who have gone before us and stand as bright lighthouses drawing us toward the Father, the source of all wisdom. Christian wisdom is founded on the same truth as natural wisdom, but it clarifies for us how to "know the difference" between when we should "let go and let God" and when we should act courageously.

∞

Heavenly Father, you know I want to do the right thing. You know I want to love as you love, to serve as you serve. You know, too, that there are people in my life who I find hard to love. I ask you to give me a heart like yours so that, beginning today, I will put people—all people—above all things, especially above those things that get in the way of loving others as you love me.

CONCLUSION

"One day at a time."

"Today, I'm sober."

"It's been eight and a half years to the day since I had my last drink."

I'm sure you have heard these or similar comments from recovering addicts. They know they are one bad choice away from their old life of chaos and misery. Every day is a journey. They never claim ultimate victory.

Whether we struggle with addiction or not, being unwilling to claim final victory in our spiritual journey is profoundly healthy. The way of serenity is not a static formula that, once understood, spits out cure-all results. Although we are at the end of this book, we are just beginning. We have identified the right highway and begun moving slowly in the right direction. We have tried with varying degrees of success, I'm sure, to let go of some things we cannot change and to take on other things we previously feared were just too much to handle. Each of these attempts has been important, but thankfully, growth in the spiritual life is not determined by the success of those attempts. It is determined, rather, by God's grace, which he can deliver whenever and however he wills. In other words, even if we don't feel like we are progressing at the speed we would like, we don't need to fear or lose heart. All God asks of us is to keep moving. This journey is as long as life, and it is lined with unique street signs, designed and placed by God, that correspond perfectly to the twists and turns, the bumps and bruises, that God allows to come our way. With the background we now have, and with renewed determination to do God's will, when we see these signs we will know they are there for our own good. God is with us, and his ways and timing are perfect.

This firm determination to keep going forward without knowing how God will get us to the place of inner peace, serenity, and courage we seek makes ultimate sense because we believe in heaven and we believe that God is leading us there!

I have no idea what heaven will look like. I've got a very strong hunch, though, that it will include the best versions of the things and people I love most on earth. That's not wild speculation. Salvation history, as read in the Bible and in our own lives, is the story of God patiently—ever so patiently—revealing himself to us and wooing us toward a loving relationship with him so that we might choose by faith to be with him forever. The backdrop of this divine love story is our contact with his creation. The beauty of nature, our deep friendships with good people, the development of human reason, and, dare I add, good food, good art, good music, and good fun . . . all are pieces of God's creation, and when we use them well, they all point us to him as the source of all goodness and truth. The fact that God would take the form of his creation with the incarnation of Jesus Christ is the ultimate evidence that his creation is very, very good.

If God's creation is that good, don't you think it's unlikely that it will all pass away completely, with nothing like it in its place? It's true that the new heaven and earth foretold in the Revelation to John (21:1) will be very different from the fractured, broken reality we know now. But no great food in heaven?! Really?! As I said, I think it only makes sense—in spiritual terms—that heaven will be full of the best versions of our favorite things.

Much more importantly, if we answer affirmatively his loving call to be with him forever, heaven will be full of the best versions of ourselves and of the people whom we love. If you want to get excited about heaven, take a moment to imagine being with all of your favorite people, not as they are now but rather as fully the people God created them to be. Imagine them in perfect health of mind, body, and soul, fully in love with God, and in perfect harmony with everyone else. Now imagine a human family living in the presence of God with no envy, anger, anxiety, rancor, or fear. That's heaven!

I bring up heaven again here, in conclusion, because this way of serenity can lead us there. And getting to heaven is what matters most in life. Jesus warned us that the gate is narrow and the road is hard that leads to life (Matthew 7:14). It's hard to get to heaven, and it's hard because it's easier to follow our base passions and to live for ourselves. It's easier to be anxious about things we can't change than to accept them by learning to trust in God's providence. It's easier to allow fear and laziness to freeze us than to courageously change the things we can and should change. It's easier to follow our whims than to learn wisdom by seeking and doing the will of God.

Let's do it, then. Let's push on. Let's trust in the way of serenity that the Lord has mapped out for us in the Gospels and in his life. "I have come that you might have life, and have it in abundance" (John 10:10).

I hope this book has been for you a very small part of God's very big plan to give you everything you need to get to heaven, while having a lot of fun along the way. Writing it has certainly been both of those things for me.

NOTES

Chapter 1: A Peace That Comes from God

1. Bishop Fulton J. Sheen, *Peace of Soul* (Garden City, NY: Doubleday, 1954), 1.
2. Jean-Pierre de Caussade. *Abandonment to Divine Providence*, also titled "The Sacrament of the Present Moment," posthumously published in 1861.
3. Karl Adam, *Christ Our Brother* (New York: Macmillan, 1931).

Chapter 2: Safe from All Distress

1. "I Offer My Life," Don Moen and Clair Cloninger.

Chapter 5: God Never Leaves Us Alone

1. Joseph Ratzinger, *Introduction to Christianity*, 2nd ed. (1969; reprint, San Francisco: Ignatius Press, 1990, 2004), II-1.

Chapter 6: If God Can Change It, Why Doesn't He?

1. Augustine, *Enchiridion on Faith, Hope, and Charity*, viii.
2. Joseph Ratzinger, *Introduction to Christianity*, 2nd ed. (1969; reprint, San Francisco: Ignatius Press, 1990, 2004), II, II, 2, c, 2.

Chapter 7: We Have Everything We Need

1. Saint Augustine, Sermon VI on "New Testament Lessons," in *Nicene and Post-Nicene Fathers: First Series,* vol. 6, ed. Philip Schaff (Peabody, MA: Hendrickson Publishers, 1994), 276.

Chapter 8: The Allure of Material Possessions

1. Saint John of the Cross, *Ascent of Mount Carmel*, ch. XI, no. 4.

Chapter 9: Climb a Mountain, Then Look Again

1. Saint Teresa of Ávila, *The Book of Her Foundations*, 5.8.

Chapter 10: Serenity Is Possible No Matter What Comes Our Way

1. Thom Peters Recovery Blog: http://www.tpetersrecovery.blogspot.com/.
2. Saint Augustine, from a commentary on the Psalms.
3. Prayer attributed to St. Thomas Aquinas (1225–1274).

Chapter 11: Owning Our History

1. Saint Augustine, *Confessions,* Book 8, ch. 17.

Chapter 12: God Loves You, Warts and All

1. Pope John Paul II, World Youth Day 2002, homily at outdoor Mass, Toronto (July 28, 2002). http://www.vatican.va/holy_father/john_paul_ii/homilies/2002/documents/hf_jp-ii_hom_20020728_xvii-wyd_en.html.

Chapter 13: God's Mercy Has No Limits

1. *Saint Therese of Lisieux: Her Last Conversations,* November 7, 1897, no. 6.
2. Saint Francis de Sales, *Introduction to the Devout Life,* ch. 19.

Chapter 14: Gratitude as a Path to Peace

1. Though the Book of Judith does not belong to the official canon of the Jewish scriptures, it formed part of the Septuagint Greek translation of the Bible, and many Jewish scholars consider it to be a worthy description of the background events leading up to the Jewish holiday of Hanukkah.
2. Although it has different historical roots, a feast of thanksgiving is celebrated by Canadians as well; the Canadian Thanksgiving is held on the second Monday of October, the day established in 1957 by the Canadian Parliament.
3. George Washington, Proclamation of Thanksgiving, Oct. 3, 1789, at http://www.churchstatelaw.com/historicalmaterials/8_6_2_1.asp.

Chapter 15: It's All About Joy

1. George Washington, Proclamation of Thanksgiving, Oct. 3, 1789 at http://www.churchstatelaw.com/historicalmaterials/8_6_2_1.asp.

Chapter 16: Can We Really Make a Difference?

1. Voltaire, "La Bégueule," which begins: "Dans ses écrits, un sage Italien, dit que le mieux est l'ennemi du bien."
2. One of my favorite theologians, Hans Urs von Balthasar, repeatedly invited us to live joyfully because we have great reason for hope, no matter what situation we find ourselves in. He said that amid all the fear that characterizes the times we live in, we have every reason to live in joy and to communicate this joy to others, because Christ has already been victorious over sin and death.

Chapter 18: Some Change Is Necessary

1. Saint Augustine, *Confessions,* Book 8, ch. 5.
2. Frances Hodgson Burnett, *The Land of the Blue Flower* (1904), http://www.online-literature.com/burnett/3041/.

Chapter 20: You've Got a Big Part in the Play

1. Pope John Paul II, post-synodal apostolic exhortation Reconciliatio et Paenitentia (Dec. 2, 1984), no. 4.

Chapter 21: In God's Eyes, We Are All Action Figures

1. Pope John Paul II, *Post-Synodal Apostolic Exhortation Christifideles Laici* (1981), no. 3.
2. Pope Benedict XVI, *Encyclical Letter Deus Caritas Est* (2005), no. 31c.
3. Second Vatican Council, *Dogmatic Constitution on the Church Lumen Gentium* (1964), no. 31.

Chapter 24: Blessed Are the Merciful

1. Pope John Paul II, *Encyclical Letter Dives in Misericordia* (1980), no. 12.

Chapter 27: The Courage to Get Back Up After Falling

1. Maximilian Kolbe, *Stronger Than Hatred: A Collection of Spiritual Writings,* 2nd ed. (Hyde Park, NY: New City Press, 1988).

Chapter 31: Cultivating Our Interior Life

1. See Plato, *Apology,* 38a.

Chapter 32: Spiritual but Not Religious?

1. Pope John Paul II, *Crossing the Threshold of Hope* (New York: Alfred A. Knopf, 1994), p. 31.
2. Saint Augustine, Confessions (397 AD), p. 1.

Chapter 33: The Whispers of God

1. This homily is attributed to the writer now known as Pseudo-Chrysostom.

Chapter 34: The Root of All Wisdom

1. Niccolò Machiavelli, *The Prince,* ch. 17.
2. Saint Augustine, *De Gratia et Libero Arbitrio,* xviii.

Chapter 36: Don't Avoid Risks, Take the Right Ones

1. *Catechism of the Catholic Church* (1992), no. 1806.

Chapter 37: A Life of Purpose and Meaning

1. Viktor E. Frankl, *Man's Search for Meaning* (New York: Simon & Schuster, 1985), 157.
2. Frankl, *Man's Search for Meaning,* 126.

Chapter 38: Christian Wisdom?

1. C. S. Lewis, "Christianity and Literature," in *Christian Reflections* (Grand Rapids, MI: Eerdmans, 1967), 1–11.

Chapter 39: I've Got Heaven on My Mind

1. Suzy Welch, *10-10-10: A Life-Transforming Idea* (New York: Scribner, 2009).
2. Thomas à Kempis, *The Imitation of Christ,* book I, ch. 23.